40 Colorful AFGHANS to Crochet

40 Colorful AFGHANS to Crochet

A collection of eye-popping stitch patterns, blocks & projects

Leonie Morgan

ST. MARTIN'S GRIFFIN
NEW YORK

40 Colorful Afghans to Crochet

Library of Congress Cataloging-in-
Publication Data Available Upon Request

ISBN: 978-1-250-12506-4 (trade paperback)
ISBN: 978-1-250-12507-1 (e-edition)

Our books may be purchased in bulk for
promotional, educational, or business use.
Please contact your local bookseller or
the Macmillan Corporate and Premium
Sales Department at (800) 221-7945,
extension 5442, or by e-mail at
MacmillanSpecialMarkets@macmillan.com.

First U.S. Edition: July 2017

10 9 8 7 6 5 4 3 2 1

Conceived, designed, and produced by
Quarto Publishing plc
The Old Brewery
6 Blundell Street
London N7 9BH
www.quartoknows.com

QUAR.STPA

Editors: Lily de Gatacre, Michelle Pickering
Senior art editor: Emma Clayton
Layout designer: Jo Bettles
Photographers: Nicki Dowey, Phil Wilkins
Pattern checker: Therese Chynoweth
Chart illustrations: Kuo Kang Chen
Editorial assistant: Danielle Watt
Designer: Martina Calvio
Art director: Caroline Guest
Creative director: Moira Clinch
Publisher: Sam Warrington

Color separation by PICA Digital Pte Ltd,
Singapore

Printed by 1010 Printing International Ltd,
China

Contents

Welcome

Turning a strand of yarn into a crochet design is always a journey of exploration for me. I never quite know what I'll make until my hands begin to move. Sometimes I have a vague idea in mind before I start to crochet, but more often it's a complete mystery to me. My hands move, stitches appear, and before long I've designed something—not always perfect to start with, but something that I can tweak and develop into a pattern.

My favorite designs are patterns that can be used for afghans, be they square blocks or row-by-row designs. Afghans are my favorite sort of project to have on the go in my yarn basket. Bit by bit, the squares add up to a tottering pile of colorful loveliness, or the afghan steadily grows as each row is added. There is nothing more satisfying in the crochet world (besides the obvious deliciousness of buying new yarn) than weaving in the last horrid yarn end of an afghan you've made. Nestling under the freshly made and gorgeous crochet blanket gives you a feeling of very smug satisfaction!

In this book I've gathered 40 fab patterns to crochet into afghans. Half of the designs are block patterns and the other half are row-by-row patterns, so you have a choice of what sort of afghan to make. For each of the designs, you will find yarn quantities for making blankets in three different sizes at the back of the book, so you can get crocheting straightaway.

I hope this book will give you lots of happy crocheting time and inspiration, and help you to experience the wonderful feeling of completing an afghan of your own.

Happy Hooking!

Leonie Morgan

About This Book

This book is an eye-catching resource of afghan patterns for you to crochet. As well as the 40 main designs, there are 12 edging patterns to give your afghan the perfect finish. At the end of the book you will find information on techniques and yarn quantities.

Edgings, pages 100–109

There are 12 edging designs to help you finish your afghan perfectly.

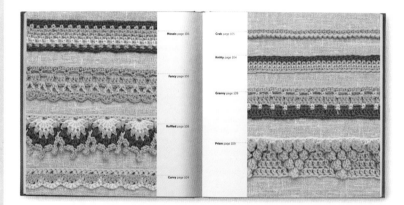

Techniques, pages 110–123

An illustrated, comprehensive, and concise guide provides everything you need to know to get started crocheting the afghans. At the end of the book you will also find a list of yarn quantities for making three different sizes of afghan using each of the main designs.

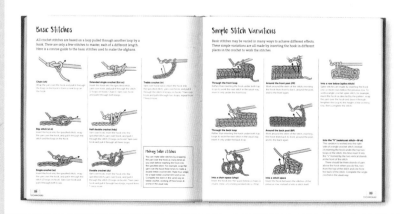

Afghan Collection, pages 8–99

At the heart of this book are the 40 afghan designs. With written patterns, charts, and clear photographs taking you through each design, you will want to start crocheting right away.

■ Five of the patterns have been made into full-size finished afghans to inspire you.

■ Instructions for any special stitches used in each design are provided alongside the pattern.

Skill level gives a rough guide to difficulty:
1 = easy
2 = intermediate
3 = advanced

Hook size and type of yarn used to make the sample shown.

Half of the patterns are block designs and half are row-by-row designs.

Gauge information is provided as either the finished size of a single block or the number of stitches and rows to a given size.

Additional information lists any special techniques used and whether the design is reversible (the same on both sides).

List of yarn colors for each design. Quantities are provided for making a single block or the full-size afghan shown. Refer also to page 124 for yarn quantities for three different sizes of afghan.

A key to the symbols used in the charts is provided for each design.

A written pattern takes you through the pattern round by round or row by row.

Alternating colors in the charts indicate each round or row.

As a bonus, there are 12 edging designs to help you finish your afghan perfectly.

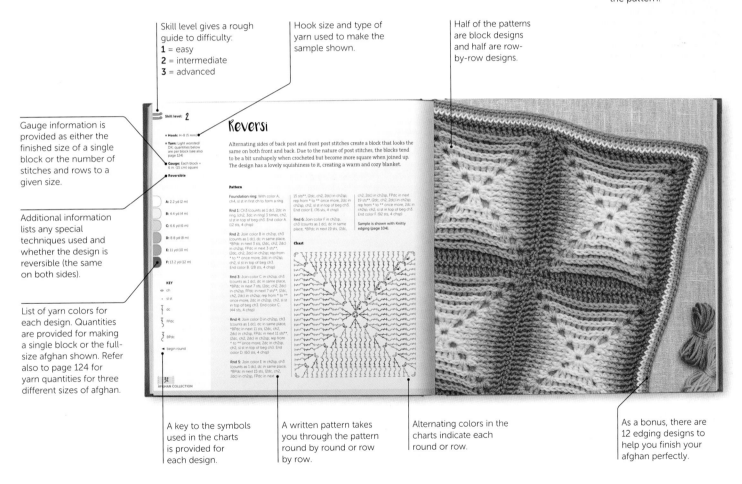

Afghan Collection

On the following pages you will find 40 bright and colorful afghan patterns. Split into 20 block designs and 20 row-by-row designs, and ranging from beginner to advanced level, there is plenty to choose from. Check page 124 for yarn quantities for three different sizes of afghan for each pattern.

- **Hook:** H-8 (5 mm)

- **Yarn:** Light worsted/ DK (see page 124 for quantities)

- **Gauge:** 14 sts and 13 rows in pattern = 4 in. (10 cm) square

A

B

C

D

E

F

G

H

KEY

o ch

+ sc

T hdc

Ť dc

⬮ bobble

◄ begin row

Bobble Along

Bands of aligned and staggered bobbles surrounded by rows of simple stitches create a warm and tactile afghan. The dense stitching also makes this pattern especially suitable for baby blankets.

Pattern

Foundation row: With color A, ch a multiple of 2 + 2 + 3 turning ch.

Row 1 (RS): Beg in 5th ch from hook (first ch3 counts as 1 dc), dc in each ch to end. End color A. Turn.

Row 2 (WS): Join color B, ch1, sc in each st to end. End color B. Turn.

Row 3: Join color C, ch2 (counts as 1 hdc), hdc in each st to end. End color C. Turn.

Row 4: Repeat row 2 using color D. End color D. Turn.

Row 5: Repeat row 2 using color E. Do not end color E. Turn.

Row 6: Ch1, sc in first st, [sc in next st, BO in next st] to last st, sc in last st. End color E. Turn.

Row 7: Repeat row 2 using color F. Do not end color F. Turn.

Row 8: Ch1, sc in first st, [BO in next st, sc in next st] to last st, sc in last st. End color F. Turn.

Rows 9 + 10: Repeat rows 5 + 6 using color G. End color G. Turn.

Rows 11 + 12: Repeat rows 7 + 8 using color H. End color H. Do not turn.

Row 13: Join color D in first st of last row and repeat row 2. End color D. Turn.

Row 14: Repeat row 3 using color C. End color C. Turn.

Row 15: Repeat row 2 using color B. End color B. Turn.

Row 16: Join color A, ch3 (counts as 1 dc), dc in each st to end. End color A. Turn.

Row 17: Repeat row 5 using color G. End color G. Turn.

Rows 18 + 19: Repeat rows 7 + 8 using color F. End color F. Turn.

Rows 20 + 21: Repeat rows 18 + 19 using color C. End color C. Turn.

Rows 22 + 23: Repeat rows 18 + 19 using color H. End color H. Do not turn.

Row 24: Join color G in first st of last row and repeat row 2. Turn.

Row 25: Repeat row 16 using color A. End color A. Turn.

Repeat rows 2–25 until fabric is the desired length.

Chart

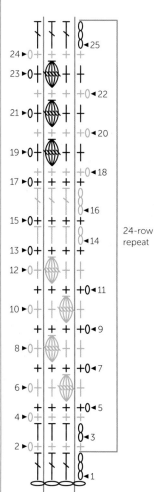

24-row repeat

2-st repeat

SPECIAL STITCH

Bobble (BO):
Work 5dc in place indicated but omit final yo of each dc, yo and pull through all 6 loops on hook.

Skill level: 3

- **Hook:** H-8 (5 mm)
- **Yarn:** Light worsted/DK (see page 124 for quantities)
- **Gauge:** 9 sts and 8 rows = 4 in. (10 cm) square

A
B
C
D
E
F
G
H

KEY

o	ch
+	sc
T	hdc
⋏	hdc2tog
⅄	beg CL
⋏	CL
	bead stitch
♡	surface crochet heart
◄	begin row

Band of Hearts

Rows of half double crochet and cluster stitches create a soft, squidgy afghan, while bands of surface crochet and bead stitch hearts add interest and color.

Pattern

Foundation row: With color A, loosely ch a multiple of 4 + 2 + 1 turning ch.

Row 1 (RS): Sc in 2nd ch from hook, hdc in next ch, [hdc2tog] to end, hdc in last ch. End color A. Turn.

Row 2 (WS): Join color B, ch1, sc in first st, hdc in next st, [hdc2tog] to end, hdc in last st. End color B. Turn.

Row 3: Repeat row 2 using color C. End color C. Do not turn.

Row 4: Join color D, beg CL in first st, *CL in each of next 2 sts, ch1, CL in each of next 2 sts; rep from * to last st, CL in last st. End color D. Do not turn.

Surface crochet hearts: With RS facing, join color E in first ch1sp on right-hand side of row 4, work surface crochet heart; rep in each ch1sp to end, alternating colors E and C. Turn.

Rows 5–7: Repeat row 2 using color F, then color G, then color A.

Row 8: Repeat row 4 using color D. End color D. Do not turn.

Row 9: Join color H, ch4 (counts as 1 dc, ch1), *skip 2 sts, (BS, ch1, BS) in ch1sp, skip 2 sts**, ch3; rep

from * to last 5 sts, rep from * to ** once, ch1, dc in last st. End color H. Do not turn.

Row 10: Join color D in 3rd ch of beg ch4 of row 9, ch1 and sc in same place, *working behind row 9 and into row 8: CL in next st, dc in next 2 sts, CL in next st; rep from * to last st, sc in last st of row 9. End color D. Do not turn.

Row 11: Join color D in first sc of last row, beg CL in first st, CL in each st to end. End color D. Turn.

Rows 12–14: Repeat row 2 using color A, then color G, then color F.

Row 15: Join color D and repeat row 4. Do not turn.

Surface crochet hearts: With RS facing, join color C in first ch1sp on right-hand side of row 15, work surface crochet heart; rep in each ch1sp to end, alternating colors C and E. Do not turn.

Row 16: Join color A in first st of last row and repeat row 2. End color A. Turn.

Repeat rows 2–16 until fabric is the desired length.

Chart

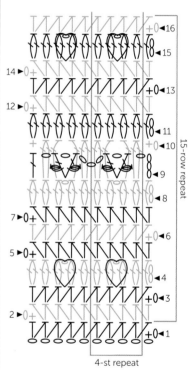

15-row repeat

4-st repeat

Surface crochet heart

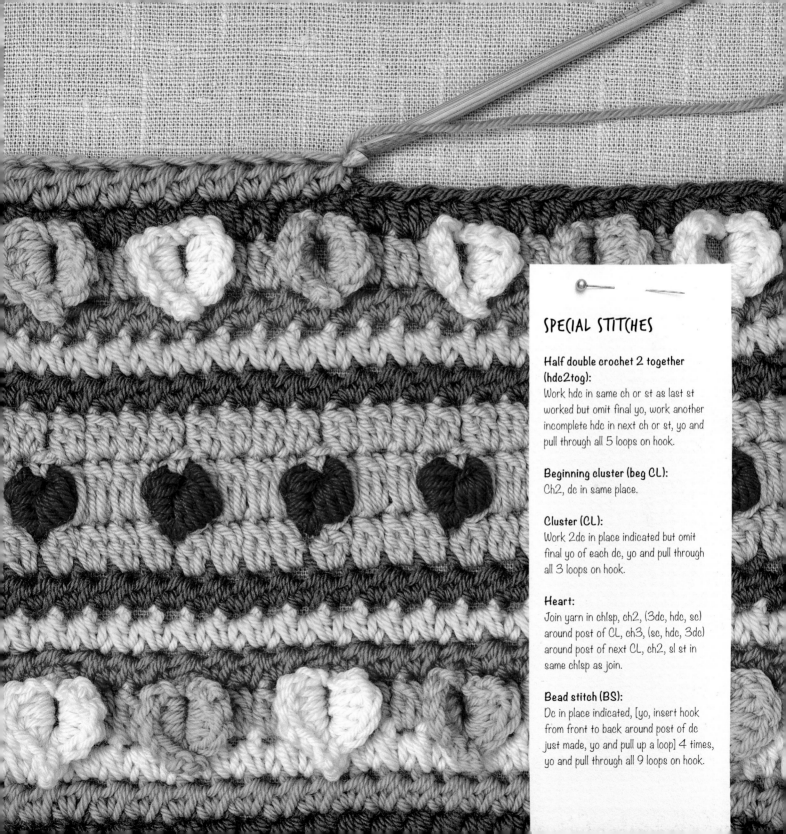

SPECIAL STITCHES

Half double crochet 2 together (hdc2tog):
Work hdc in same ch or st as last st worked but omit final yo, work another incomplete hdc in next ch or st, yo and pull through all 5 loops on hook.

Beginning cluster (beg CL):
Ch2, dc in same place.

Cluster (CL):
Work 2dc in place indicated but omit final yo of each dc, yo and pull through all 3 loops on hook.

Heart:
Join yarn in chlsp, ch2, (3dc, hdc, sc) around post of CL, ch3, (sc, hdc, 3dc) around post of next CL, ch2, sl st in same chlsp as join.

Bead stitch (BS):
Dc in place indicated, [yo, insert hook from front to back around post of dc just made, yo and pull up a loop] 4 times, yo and pull through all 9 loops on hook.

- **Hook:** J-10 (6 mm)

- **Yarn:** Light worsted/ DK (see page 124 for quantities)

- **Gauge:** 12 sts and 24 rows = 3½ in. (9 cm) wide x 4¼ in. (11 cm) high

- **Crochet technique:** Tapestry (page 119)

- **Reversible**

A

B

C

D

Baby Diamonds

Baby Diamonds is a tapestry crochet pattern, so the stitches are close fitting and create a thick, warm fabric. It has an almost woven texture that is perfect for babies and little baby fingers. For a neat finish, insert the hook under the carried strand of yarn when working the stitches, and join new colors at the start of the row.

Chart

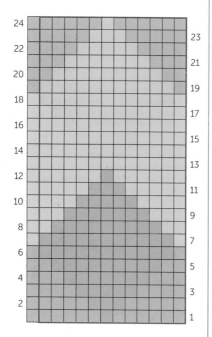

Pattern

Foundation row: With color A, ch a multiple of 12 + 1 + 1 turning ch.

Working from chart: Start at the bottom right-hand corner of the chart and work in single crochet, beginning the first row in the 2nd ch from hook. Each square represents 1 stitch. Right-side rows are read from right to left and wrong-side rows are read from left to right. Remember to ch1 at the beginning of each row for a turning ch (this does not count as a stitch).

To change to a different color: Join the new color required at the beginning of the row, hold the new (or unused) color along the top edge, and work single crochet over it until it is needed. To change from one color to another, work to 1 stitch before the color change. Begin this stitch normally, working to the last yarn over, then drop the current color to the wrong side of the work, pick up the new color, and use it to complete the stitch.

Pattern repeat: The section highlighted in red on the chart is the pattern repeat. Repeat this section until you have 1 stitch remaining on right-side rows, then work the last stitch at the left edge of the chart. On wrong-side rows, work the first stitch, then repeat the highlighted section to the end of the row.

- **Hook:** H-8 (5 mm)
- **Yarn:** Light worsted/ DK; quantities below are per block (see also page 124)
- **Gauge:** Each block = 6 in. (15 cm) square

A: 1.7 yd (1.5 m)

B: 2.8 yd (2.5 m)

C: 7.2 yd (6.5 m)

D: 14.3 yd (13 m)

E: 8.8 yd (8 m)

KEY

o	ch
•	sl st
+	sc
T	hdc
T	dc
beg CL symbol	beg CL
CL symbol	CL
◄	begin round

Dazzling Daisy

This cheerful crochet block would look fantastic in lots of different colorways. The pattern has one round of cluster stitches but is otherwise an easy pattern. Try working the flowers in bright colors and the borders in a neutral color, or you could work round 3 in a fluffier yarn for added texture.

Pattern

Foundation ring: With color A, ch4, sl st in first ch to form a ring.

Rnd 1: Ch3 (counts as 1 dc), 11dc in ring, sl st in top of beg ch3. End color A. (12 sts)

Rnd 2: Join color B, ch5 (counts as 1 dc, ch2), [dc in next st, ch2] 11 times, sl st in 3rd ch of beg ch5. End color B. (12 sts, 12 chsp)

Rnd 3: Join color C in ch2sp, beg CL in same place, [ch3, CL in next ch2sp] 11 times, ch3, sl st in top of beg CL. End color C. (12 CL, 12 chsp)

Rnd 4: Join color D in ch3sp, ch1, [4sc in ch3sp] 12 times, sl st in first sc made. End color D. (48 sts)

Rnd 5: Join color E in first sc in any group of 4sc, ch3 (counts as 1 dc), *2dc in next st, ch2, 2dc in next st, dc in next st, hdc in next st, sc in next 6 sts, hdc in next st**, dc in next st; rep from * twice more, then from * to ** once, sl st in top of beg ch3. (56 sts, 4 chsp)

Rnd 6: Sl st in each st to corner ch2sp, ch3 (counts as 1 dc), (dc, ch2, 2dc) in same place, [dc in each st to next corner ch2sp, (2dc, ch2, 2dc) in ch2sp] 3 times,

dc in each st to end, sl st in top of beg ch3. End color E. (72 sts, 4 chsp)

Rnd 7: Join color D in ch2sp, ch1, [(sc, hdc, sc) in ch2sp, sc in next 18 sts] 4 times, sl st in first sc made. End color D. (84 sts)

Chart

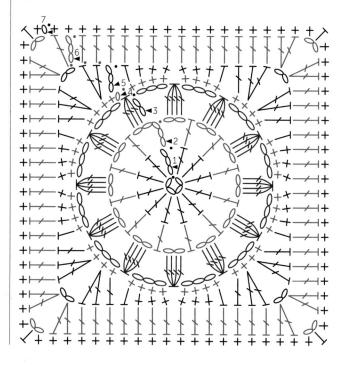

SPECIAL STITCHES

Beginning cluster (beg CL):
Ch2, work 3dc in place indicated but omit final yo of each dc, yo and pull through all 4 loops on hook.

Cluster (CL):
Work 4dc in place indicated but omit final yo of each dc, yo and pull through all 5 loops on hook.

- **Hook:** H-8 (5 mm)
- **Yarn:** Light worsted/ DK; quantities below are per block (see also page 124)
- **Gauge:** Each block = 6 in. (15 cm) square

A: 1.7 yd (1.5 m)

B: 10.4 yd (9.5 m)

C: 2.2 yd (2 m)

D: 8.8 yd (8 m)

E: 3.3 yd (3 m)

F: 3.9 yd (3.5 m)

G: 4.4 yd (4 m)

KEY

o	ch
•	sl st
+	sc
T	hdc
⊤	dc
◄	begin row or round

Granny's Corner

An alternative to the traditional granny square, this block is worked from corner to corner. This is another great stash-busting pattern, or you could use different colors for even-numbered rows and one neutral color for odd-numbered rows. All rows and rounds are worked from the right side.

Pattern

Foundation ring: With color A, ch4, sl st in first ch to form a ring.

Row 1: Ch3 (counts as 1 dc), (3dc, ch2, 4dc) in ring. End color A. (8 sts, 1 chsp)

Row 2: Join color B in first st of last row, ch1 and sc in same place, ch2, skip 3 sts, (sc, ch3, sc) in ch2sp, ch2, skip 3 sts, sc in last st. End color B. (4 sts, 3 chsp)

Row 3: Join color C in first st of last row, ch3 (counts as 1 dc), 3dc in ch2sp, (3dc, ch2, 3dc) in ch3sp, 3dc in ch2sp, dc in last st. End color C. (14 sts, 1 chsp)

Chart

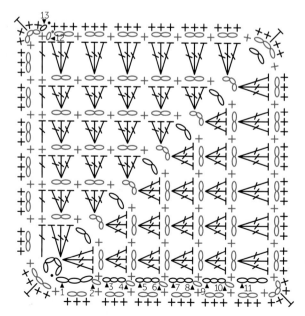

Row 4: Join color B in first st of last row, ch1 and sc in same place, ch2, skip 3 sts, sc in gap before next st, ch2, skip 3 sts, (sc, ch3, sc) in ch2sp, ch2, skip 3 sts, sc in gap before next st, ch2, skip 3 sts, sc in last st. End color B. (6 sts, 5 chsp)

Row 5: Join color D in first st of last row, ch3 (counts as 1 dc), [3dc in next ch2sp] twice, (3dc, ch2, 3dc) in ch3sp, [3dc in next ch2sp] twice, dc in last st. End color D. (20 sts, 1 chsp)

Row 6: Join color B in first st of last row, ch1 and sc in same place, [ch2, skip 3 sts, sc in gap before next st] twice, ch2, skip 3 sts, (sc, ch3, sc) in ch2sp, [ch2, skip 3 sts, sc in gap before next st] twice, ch2, skip 3 sts, sc in last st. End color B. (8 sts, 7 chsp)

Row 7: Join color E in first st of last row, ch3 (counts as 1 dc), [3dc in next ch2sp] 3 times, (3dc, ch2, 3dc) in ch3sp, [3dc in next ch2sp] 3 times, dc in last st. End color E. (26 sts, 1 chsp)

Row 8: Join color B in first st of last row, ch1 and sc in same place, [ch2, skip 3 sts, sc in gap before next st] 3 times, ch2, skip 3 sts, (sc, ch3, sc) in ch2sp, [ch2, skip 3 sts, sc in gap before next st] 3 times, ch2, skip 3 sts, sc in last st. End color B. (10 sts, 9 chsp)

Row 9: Join color F in first st of last row, ch3 (counts as 1 dc), [3dc in next ch2sp] 4 times, (3dc, ch2, 3dc) in ch3sp, [3dc in next ch2sp] 4 times, dc in last st. End color F. (32 sts, 1 chsp)

Row 10: Join color B in first st of last row, ch1 and sc in same place, [ch2, skip 3 sts, sc in gap before next st] 4 times, ch2, skip 3 sts, (sc, ch3, sc) in ch2sp, [ch2, skip 3 sts, sc in gap before next st] 4 times, ch2, skip 3 sts, sc in last st. End color B. (12 sts, 11 chsp)

Row 11: Join color G in first st of last row, ch3 (counts as 1 dc), [3dc in next ch2sp] 5 times, (3dc, ch2, 3dc) in ch3sp, [3dc in next ch2sp] 5 times, dc in last st. End color G. (38 sts, 1 chsp)

Edging

Rnd 12: Join color B in last st made, ch1, (sc, ch3, sc) in same place, [ch2, sc in side of next sc along edge of block] 5 times, ch2, (sc, ch3, sc) in foundation ring, [ch2, sc in side of next sc along

edge of block] 5 times, ch2, (sc, ch3, sc) in top of first st on row 11, [ch2, skip 3 sts, sc in gap before next st] 5 times, ch2, (sc, ch3, sc) in ch2sp, [ch2, skip 3 sts, sc in gap before next st] 5 times, ch2, sl st in first sc made. End color B. (28 sts, 28 chsp)

Rnd 13: Join color D in ch3sp, ch1, *(2sc, hdc, 2sc) in ch3sp, [3sc in next ch2sp] 6 times; rep from * 3 times more, sl st in first sc made. End color D. (92 sts)

- **Hook:** H-8 (5 mm)

- **Yarn:** Light worsted/
DK; quantities below
are per block (see also
page 124)

- **Gauge:** Each block =
6 in. (15 cm) square

- **Crochet technique:**
Intarsia (page 119)

- **Reversible**

A: 14.3 yd (13 m)

B: 3.3 yd (3 m)

C: 2.2 yd (2 m)

D: 7.7 yd (7 m)

E: 7.7 yd (7 m)

Interrupted

This colorwork block is very easy to crochet. The stitches are close fitting, making it ideal for baby blankets. Try laying the squares out in different directions to create interesting patterns. You could also turn the block into a blanket pattern by chaining a multiple of 22 and repeating the pattern as needed.

Pattern

Foundation row: With color A, ch22 + 1 turning ch.

Working from chart: Start at the bottom right-hand corner of the chart and work in single crochet, beginning the first row in the 2nd ch from hook. Each square represents 1 stitch. Right-side rows are read from right to left and wrong-side rows are read from left to right. Remember to ch1 at the beginning of each row for a turning ch (this does not count as a stitch).

To change to a different color in the middle of a row: Work to 1 stitch before the color change. Begin this stitch normally, working to the last yarn over, then drop the current color to the wrong side of the work, pick up the new color, and use it to complete the stitch.

To change to a different color at the beginning of a row: Work the last stitch of the last row as for color changes in the middle of the row, then turn and ch1 with the new color.

Chart

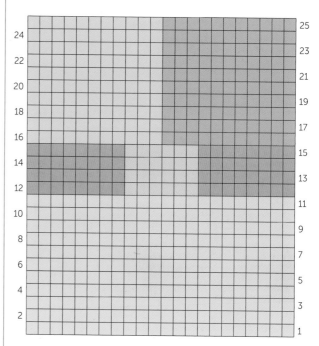

Skill level: 1

- **Hook:** H-8 (5 mm)
- **Yarn:** Light worsted/ DK; quantities below are per block (see also page 124)
- **Gauge:** Each block = 6 in. (15 cm) square
- **Reversible**

A: 2.2 yd (2 m)

B: 2.8 yd (2.5 m)

C: 3.9 yd (3.5 m)

D: 5 yd (4.5 m)

E: 6.1 yd (5.5 m)

F: 9.9 yd (9 m)

G: 12.1 yd (11 m)

KEY

o   ch

•   sl st

+   sc

◄   begin row or round

Log Cabin

Inspired by quilt designs, this block is a great way to use up scraps just like quilters do. You can lay the squares out in different ways to create color patterns.

Pattern

Foundation row: With color A, ch6.

Row 1: Beg in 2nd ch from hook, sc in next 5ch, turn. (5 sts)

Row 2: Ch1, sc in each st to end, turn.

Rows 3–5: Repeat row 2, changing to color B on last st of row 5. End color A.

Row 6: Ch1, turn work 90 degrees clockwise, sc in next 4 row ends, 3sc in first foundation ch, sc in next 4 foundation ch, turn. (11 sts)

Row 7: Ch1, sc in 5 sts, 3sc in next st, sc in 5 sts, turn. (13 sts)

Row 8: Ch1, sc in 6 sts, 3sc in next st, sc in 6 sts, changing to color C on last st. End color B. (15 sts)

Row 9: Ch1, turn work 90 degrees clockwise, sc in first 7 row ends, 3sc in next st, sc in next 4 sts and next 3 row ends, turn. (17 sts)

Row 10: Ch1, sc in 8 sts, 3sc in next st, sc in 8 sts, turn. (19 sts)

Row 11: Ch1, sc in 9 sts, 3sc in next st, sc in 9 sts, changing to color D on last st. End color C. (21 sts)

Row 12: Ch1, turn work 90 degrees clockwise, sc in next 3 row ends and next 7 sts, 3sc in next st, sc in next 7 sts and next 3 row ends, turn. (23 sts)

Row 13: Ch1, sc in 11 sts, 3sc in next st, sc in 11 sts, turn. (25 sts)

Row 14: Ch1, sc in 12 sts, 3sc in next st, sc in 12 sts, changing to color E on last st. End color D. (27 sts)

Row 15: Ch1, turn work 90 degrees clockwise, sc in next 3 row ends and next 10 sts, 3sc in next st, sc in next 10 sts and next 3 row ends, turn. (29 sts)

Chart

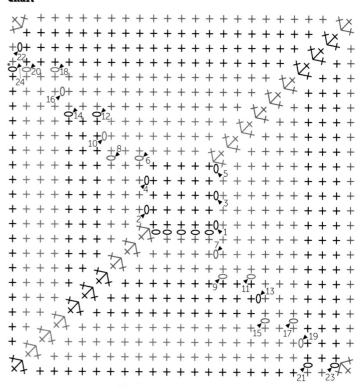

Row 16: Ch1, sc in 14 sts, 3sc in next st, sc in 14 sts, turn. (31 sts)

Row 17: Ch1, sc in 15 sts, 3sc in next st, sc in 15 sts, changing to color F on last st. End color E. (33 sts)

Row 18: Ch1, turn work 90 degrees clockwise, sc in next 3 row ends and next 13 sts, 3sc in next st, sc in next 13 sts and next 3 row ends, turn. (35 sts)

Row 19: Ch1, sc in 17 sts, 3sc in next st, sc in 17 sts, turn. (37 sts)

Row 20: Ch1, sc in 18 sts, 3sc in next st, sc in 18 sts, changing to color G on last st. End color F. (39 sts)

Row 21: Ch1, turn work 90 degrees clockwise, sc in next 3 row ends and next 16 sts, 3sc in next st, sc in next 16 sts and next 3 row ends, turn. (41 sts)

Row 22: Ch1, sc in 20 sts, 3sc in next st, sc in 20 sts, turn. (43 sts)

Row 23: Ch1, sc in 21 sts, 3sc in next st, sc in 21 sts. End color G. (45 sts)

Rnd 24 (edging): Turn work 90 degrees clockwise and join color F in first st worked in color F, ch1 and sc in same st, sc in next 18 sts, 3sc in next st, sc in next 19 sts, changing to color G on last st. Continue with color G, sc in next 2 row ends, 3sc in next st, [sc in next 21 sts, 3sc in next st] twice, sc in next 2 row ends, sl st in first sc made. End both colors. (96 sts)

Skill level: 2

- **Hook:** H-8 (5 mm)
- **Yarn:** Light worsted/DK; quantities below are for afghan shown (see also page 124)
- **Gauge:** 12 sts and 7 rows = 4 in. (10 cm) square
- **Afghan size:** 60 x 70 in. (150 x 175 cm) including edging

A: 215 yd (196 m)

B: 329 yd (300 m)

C: 307 yd (280 m)

D: 215 yd (196 m)

E: 215 yd (196 m)

F: 215 yd (196 m)

G: 215 yd (196 m)

H: 215 yd (196 m)

I: 215 yd (196 m)

J: 215 yd (196 m)

K: 215 yd (196 m)

L: 215 yd (196 m)

Holi Festival Blanket

This afghan is made with a big palette of bright colors inspired by the spice-throwing Indian festival, Holi. Rows of double crochet, granny stripes, and V-stitches make up the deceptively simple design. The only stitches used are actually double crochet and chain stitches. All rows are worked from the right side so there is no turning involved, which is great as the blanket grows in size.

Turn the page for the chart and pattern instructions.

KEY

○ ch

⊤ dc

◄ begin row or round

Pattern

Foundation row: With color A, loosely ch a multiple of 3 + 2 + 3 turning ch. To match afghan shown, ch179.

Row 1: Beg in 5th ch from hook, (first ch3 counts as 1 dc), dc in each ch to end. End color A.

Row 2: Join color B in first st of last row, ch3 (counts as 1 dc), dc in each st to end. End color B.

Row 3: Repeat row 2 using color C.

Row 4: Join color D in first st of last row, ch3 (counts as 1 dc), [skip 1 st, 3dc in next st, skip 1 st] to last st, dc in last st. End color D.

Row 5: Join color E in first st of last row, ch3 (counts as 1 dc), dc in same place, [skip 3 sts, 3dc in gap before next st] to last 4 sts, skip 3 sts, 2dc in last st. End color E.

Row 6: Join color F in first st of last row, ch3 (counts as 1 dc), skip 1 st, [3dc in gap before next st, skip 3 sts] to last 2 sts, 3dc in gap before next st, skip 1 st, dc in last st. End color F.

Row 7: Repeat row 5 using color G.

Row 8: Repeat row 6 using color H.

Row 9: Join color I in first st of last row, ch3 (counts as 1 dc), dc in each st to end. End color I.

Row 10: Join color J in first st of last row, ch3 (counts as 1 dc), [skip 1 st, V-st in next st, skip 1 st] to last st, dc in last st. End color J.

Row 11: Join color K in first st of last row, ch3 (counts as 1 dc),

[skip 1 st, V-st in ch1sp, skip 1 st] to last st, dc in last st. End color K.

Row 12: Repeat row 11 using color L.

Row 13: Join color A in first st of last row, ch3 (counts as 1 dc), [skip 1 st, 3dc in ch1sp, skip 1 st] to last st, dc in last st. End color A.

Row 14: Repeat row 9 using color B.

Repeat rows 2–14 until fabric is the desired length, changing to the next color in the established sequence (A–L) on each row. To match afghan shown, work 58 repeats across and work the row repeat 9 times in total (118 rows).

Next 2 rows: Repeat row 2 twice, using next two colors in sequence (K and L to match afghan shown).

Edging

Rnd 1: Join color C in top-right corner st, ch1, (sc, hdc, sc) in corner st, sc in each st to last st of edge, (sc, hdc, sc) in last st, [sc around post of dc, sc in base of same dc] in each row end along side, (sc, hdc, sc) in first foundation ch, sc in each ch to last ch, (sc, hdc, sc) in last ch, [sc around post of dc, sc in top of same dc] in each row end along side, sl st in first sc made. End color C.

Rnd 2: Join color B in corner hdc, ch3 (counts as 1 dc), 4dc in same place, [dc in each st to next corner hdc, 5dc in corner hdc] 3 times, dc in each st to end, sl st in top of beg ch3. End color B.

A simple double crochet edging is easy to add and gives a neat finish to the blanket.

Chart

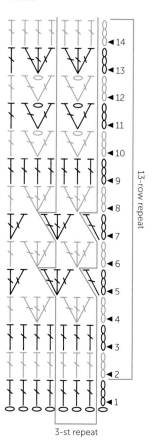

13-row repeat

3-st repeat

This rainbow blanket is perfect for relaxing on the couch all year round—celebrating the summer or bringing color and warmth to a winter evening.

SPECIAL STITCH

V-stitch (V-st):
(Dc, ch1, dc) in place indicated.

- **Hook:** H-8 (5 mm)

- **Yarn:** Light worsted/ DK (see page 124 for quantities)

- **Gauge:** 20 sts and approx. 6½ rows in dc = 4 in. (10 cm) square

A

B

C

D

KEY

o ch

ꕔ dc

◄ begin row

← direction of work

Neon Frills

This pattern is a simple eyelet fabric decorated with surface crochet. There are frills on alternate eyelet rows, but you could add frills on every eyelet row for a really frilly fabric. You could also omit the frills for a simple and very easy afghan. Use up all those scraps you have and experiment with different types of yarn for the frills.

Pattern

Foundation row: With color A, ch a multiple of 2 + 1 + 3 turning ch.

Row 1 (RS): Beg in 5th ch from hook (first ch3 counts as 1 dc), dc in each ch to end, turn.

Row 2 (WS): Ch3 (counts as 1 dc), dc in next st, [ch1, skip 1 st, dc in next st] to last st, dc in last st, turn.

Row 3: Ch3 (counts as 1 dc), dc in each st and ch1sp to end, turn.

Repeat rows 2 + 3 until fabric is the desired length, ending with a row 3. End color A.

Surface crochet frill: With RS facing, join color B, C, or D around top of post of 2nd stitch on right-hand side of row 2, ch3 (counts as 1 dc), 2dc around same post, ch1, [starting at bottom of the next st on row 2, work 3dc around post, ch1, starting at top of next st on row 2, work 3dc around post, ch1] to end of row, ending last repeat by omitting the last ch1. End color.

Work frills on every other repeat of row 2, alternating colors as desired.

Charts

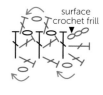

surface crochet frill

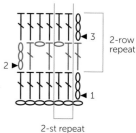

2-row repeat

2-st repeat

- **Hook:** H-8 (5 mm)

- **Yarn:** Light worsted/ DK; quantities below are per block (see also page 124)

- **Gauge:** Each block = 6 in. (15 cm) square

A: 5.5 yd (5 m)

B: 5.5 yd (5 m)

C: 5.5 yd (5 m)

D: 5.5 yd (5 m)

E: 9.9 yd (9 m)

KEY

○ ch

• sl st

+ sc

T hdc

† dc

◄ begin row or round

Pastel Rows

This is a super easy block to crochet. All rows are worked from the right side, so there is no turning involved. Experiment with laying out the squares at alternating angles to create different patterns. The block is great for using up scraps from your stash, or it can be worked in shades of one color.

Pattern

Foundation row: With color A, ch23.

Row 1: Beg in 5th ch from hook (first ch3 counts as 1 dc), dc in each ch to end. End color A. (20 sts)

Row 2: Join color B in first st of last row, ch3 (counts as 1 dc), dc in each st to end. End color B. Do not turn.

Row 3: Repeat row 2 using color C.

Row 4: Repeat row 2 using color D.

Row 5: Repeat row 2 using color B.

Row 6: Repeat row 2 using color E.

Row 7: Repeat row 2 using color A.

Row 8: Repeat row 2 using color C.

Row 9: Repeat row 2 using color D.

Edging

Rnd 10: Join color E in last st made, ch1, (sc, hdc, sc) in same place, working along side of block, [2sc around post of next st] 9 times, (sc, hdc, sc) in first foundation ch, sc in next 18 ch, (sc, hdc, sc) in next ch, [2sc around post of next st] 9 times, (sc, hdc, sc) in top of next st, sc in next 18 sts, sl st in first sc made. End color E.

Chart

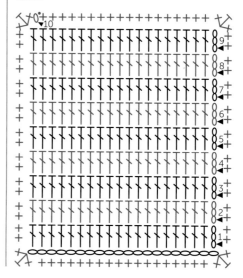

- **Hook:** H-8 (5 mm)
- **Yarn:** Light worsted/ DK; quantities below are per block (see also page 124)
- **Gauge:** Each block = 6 in. (15 cm) square
- **Reversible**

A: 2.2 yd (2 m)

B: 4.4 yd (4 m)

C: 6.6 yd (6 m)

D: 8.8 yd (8 m)

E: 11 yd (10 m)

F: 13.2 yd (12 m)

KEY

○ ch

• sl st

dc

FPdc

BPdc

◄ begin round

Reversi

Alternating sides of back post and front post stitches create a block that looks the same on both front and back. Due to the nature of post stitches, the blocks tend to be a bit unshapely when crocheted but become more square when joined up. The design has a lovely squishiness to it, creating a warm and cozy blanket.

Pattern

Foundation ring: With color A, ch4, sl st in first ch to form a ring.

Rnd 1: Ch3 (counts as 1 dc), 2dc in ring, [ch2, 3dc in ring] 3 times, ch2, sl st in top of beg ch3. End color A. (12 sts, 4 chsp)

Rnd 2: Join color B in ch2sp, ch3 (counts as 1 dc), dc in same place, *BPdc in next 3 sts, (2dc, ch2, 2dc) in ch2sp, FPdc in next 3 sts**, (2dc, ch2, 2dc) in ch2sp; rep from * to ** once more, 2dc in ch2sp, ch2, sl st in top of beg ch3. End color B. (28 sts, 4 chsp)

Rnd 3: Join color C in ch2sp, ch3 (counts as 1 dc), dc in same place, *BPdc in next 7 sts, (2dc, ch2, 2dc) in ch2sp, FPdc in next 7 sts**, (2dc, ch2, 2dc) in ch2sp; rep from * to ** once more, 2dc in ch2sp, ch2, sl st in top of beg ch3. End color C. (44 sts, 4 chsp)

Rnd 4: Join color D in ch2sp, ch3 (counts as 1 dc), dc in same place, *BPdc in next 11 sts, (2dc, ch2, 2dc) in ch2sp, FPdc in next 11 sts**, (2dc, ch2, 2dc) in ch2sp; rep from * to ** once more, 2dc in ch2sp, ch2, sl st in top of beg ch3. End color D. (60 sts, 4 chsp)

Rnd 5: Join color E in ch2sp, ch3 (counts as 1 dc), dc in same place, *BPdc in next 15 sts, (2dc, ch2, 2dc) in ch2sp, FPdc in next

15 sts**, (2dc, ch2, 2dc) in ch2sp; rep from * to ** once more, 2dc in ch2sp, ch2, sl st in top of beg ch3. End color E. (76 sts, 4 chsp)

Rnd 6: Join color F in ch2sp, ch3 (counts as 1 dc), dc in same place, *BPdc in next 19 sts, (2dc,

ch2, 2dc) in ch2sp, FPdc in next 19 sts**, (2dc, ch2, 2dc) in ch2sp; rep from * to ** once more, 2dc in ch2sp, ch2, sl st in top of beg ch3. End color F. (92 sts, 4 chsp)

Sample is shown with Knitty edging (page 104).

Chart

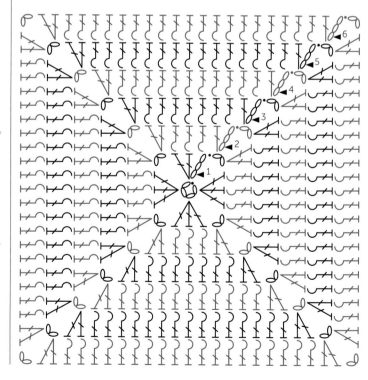

- **Hook:** J-10 (6 mm)

- **Yarn:** Light worsted/ DK (see page 124 for quantities)

- **Gauge:** Approx. 13½ sts and 13½ rows = 4 in. (10 cm) square

- **Reversible**

A

B

C

D

KEY

o ch

+ sc

⋏⋏ sc3tog

◀ begin row

Rice Field

This pattern is easy to remember and can be worked in anything from two to many colors. The stitch pattern makes a dense fabric, so use a larger hook size than you would normally. This pattern looks great on both right and wrong sides, making it a perfect design for throws. Try working the pattern in an even larger hook size for a looser texture, or use a self-striping yarn for color changes without the need to weave in ends.

Pattern

Foundation row: With color A, loosely ch a multiple of 2 + 1 + 1 turning ch.

Row 1 (RS): Sc in 2nd ch from hook, [sc3tog, ch1] to last 2 ch, sc3tog, sc in last ch. End color A. Turn.

Row 2 (WS): Join color B, ch1, sc in first st, sc3tog, [ch1, sc3tog] to end, sc in last st. End color B. Turn.

Row 3: Repeat row 2 using color C.

Row 4: Repeat row 2 using color D.

Row 5: Repeat row 2 using color A.

Repeat rows 2–5 until fabric is the desired length.

Sample is shown with Crab edging (page 105).

Chart

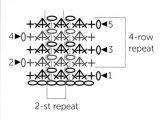

4-row repeat

2-st repeat

SPECIAL STITCH

Single crochet 3 together (sc3tog):
Insert hook in same ch or st as last st worked and draw up a loop (2 loops on hook), [insert hook in next ch or st and draw up a loop] twice (4 loops on hook), yo and pull through all 4 loops on hook.

Skill level: 3

- **Hook:** H-8 (5 mm)
- **Yarn:** Light worsted/DK (see page 124 for quantities)
- **Gauge:** Approx. 13½ sts and 12½ rows = 4 in. (10 cm) square

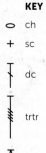

A

B

C

D

E

F

G

KEY

o   ch

+   sc

dc

trtr

trtr2tog

◄   begin row

Textured Ripple

This highly textured fabric looks like a crocheted ripple pattern, but is actually created by working stitches into previous rows. After rows 1–7, there are only two rows to remember. The sample uses a large color palette, but this design would look equally splendid in a smaller palette.

Chart

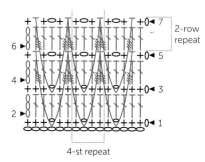

2-row repeat

4-st repeat

Pattern

Foundation row: With color A, ch a multiple of 4 + 3 + 1 turning ch.

Row 1 (RS): Sc in 2nd ch from hook, [sc in next 2 ch, ch1, skip 1 ch, sc in next ch] to last 2 ch, sc in last 2 ch, turn.

Row 2 (WS): Ch3 (counts as 1 dc), dc in each st and ch1sp to end, turn.

Row 3: Ch1, sc in first st, [sc in next 2 sts, ch1, skip 1 st, sc in next st] to last 2 sts, sc in last 2 sts, turn.

Row 4: Repeat row 2. End color A.

Row 5: Join color B, ch1, sc in first st, trtr in first skipped ch of foundation row, sc in next st, ch1, skip 1 st, sc in next st, [trtr2tog in

skipped ch just worked into and next skipped ch of foundation row, sc in next st, ch1, skip 1 st, sc in next st] to last 2 sts, trtr in last skipped ch just worked into, sc in last st, turn.

Row 6: Repeat row 2. End color B.

Row 7: Join color C, ch1, sc in first st, trtr in first skipped st 5 rows below, sc in next st, ch1, skip 1 st, sc in next st, [trtr2tog in last skipped st just worked into and next skipped st 5 rows below, sc in next st, ch1, skip 1 st, sc in next st] to last 2 sts, trtr in last skipped st just worked into, sc in last st, turn.

Row 8: Repeat row 2. End color C.

Repeat rows 7 + 8 for pattern, changing color as follows:

Rows 9 + 10: Color D.

Rows 11 + 12: Color E.

Rows 13 + 14: Color F.

Rows 15 + 16: Color G.

Continue repeating rows 7 + 8 using colors A–G in established sequence until fabric is the desired length. End with a row 7.

SPECIAL STITCHES

Triple treble (trtr):
[Yo] 4 times, insert hook in place indicated and draw up a loop (6 loops on hook), [yo and pull through 2 loops] 5 times (1 loop remains on hook).

Triple treble 2 together (trtr2tog):
[Yo] 4 times, insert hook in previous skipped st 5 rows below and draw up a loop (6 loops on hook), [yo and pull through 2 loops] 4 times (2 loops on hook), [yo] 4 times, insert hook in next skipped st 5 rows below and draw up a loop (7 loops on hook), [yo and pull through 2 loops] 4 times, yo and pull through remaining 3 loops on hook.

- **Hook:** J-10 (6 mm)
- **Yarn:** Light worsted/ DK (see page 124 for quantities)
- **Gauge:** 12½ sts and 8½ rows = 4 in. (10 cm) square
- **Reversible**

A

B

C

D

E

F

G

KEY

o ch

+ sc

⊥ Ext sc

⊗ beg PS

⊤ PS

◄ begin row

Carnival

Pineapple stitches gives this pattern a lovely, spongy feel. A rainbow palette works great for this design—the more colours, the better. The first and last rows use extended single crochet to straighten out the edges.

Pattern

Foundation row: With color A, ch a multiple of 10 + 5 + 1 turning ch.

Row 1: Beg in 2nd ch from hook, [Ext sc in next 5 ch, PS in next 5 ch] to last 5 ch, Ext sc in last 5 ch. End color A. Turn.

Row 2: Join color B, beg PS in first st, PS in next 4 sts, [sc in next 5 PS, PS in next 5 sts] to end. End color B. Turn.

Row 3: Join color C, ch1, [sc in first 5 sts, PS in next 5 sts] to last 5 sts, sc in last 5 sts. End color C. Turn.

Repeat rows 2 + 3 in the following color sequence, working 1 row of each color: color D, color E, color F, color G.

Continue repeating rows 2 + 3 using colors A–G in established sequence until fabric is the desired length. End with a row 2.

SPECIAL STITCHES

Extended single crochet (Ext sc):

Insert hook in place indicated and draw up a loop (2 loops on hook), ch1, yo and pull through both loops on hook.

Beginning pineapple stitch (beg PS):

Ch2, yo, insert hook in place indicated and draw up a loop (3 loops on hook), [yo and pull through 2 loops on hook] twice.

Pineapple stitch (PS):

[Yo, insert hook in place indicated and draw up a loop] twice (5 loops on hook), yo and pull through 4 loops on hook, yo and pull through remaining 2 loops on hook.

Chart

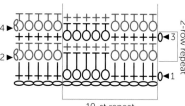

2-row repeat

10-st repeat

- **Hook:** J-10 (6 mm)

- **Yarn:** Light worsted/ DK (see page 124 for quantities)

- **Gauge:** Approx. 13½ sts and 16 rows = 4 in. (10 cm) square

- **Crochet technique:** Intarsia (page 119)

- **Reversible**

A

B

Checkmate

This simple checkerboard pattern looks great from both sides. You could work the design in more than two colors. Try winding the necessary amount of yarn to work each square onto bobbins or pegs to help stop the yarn from tangling.

Pattern

Foundation row: With color A, ch a multiple of 20 + 1 turning ch.

Working from chart: Start at the bottom right-hand corner of the chart and work in single crochet, beginning the first row in the 2nd ch from hook. Each square represents 1 stitch. Right-side rows are read from right to left and wrong-side rows are read from left to right. Remember to ch1 at the beginning of each row for a turning ch (this does not count as a stitch).

To change to a different color in the middle of a row: Work to 1 stitch before the color change. Begin this stitch normally, working to the last yarn over, then drop the current color to the wrong side of the work, pick up the new color, and use it to complete the stitch.

To change to a different color at the beginning of a row: Work the last stitch of the last row as for color changes in the middle of the row, then turn and ch1 with the new color.

Chart

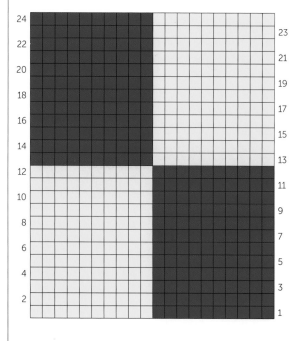

- **Hook:** H-8 (5 mm)

- **Yarn:** Light worsted/ DK; quantities below are per block (see also page 124)

- **Gauge:** Each block = 6 in. (15 cm) square

- **Afghan size:** 36 in. (90 cm) square; 36 blocks joined in 6 rows of 6 blocks

A: 3.9 yd (3.5 m)

B: 18.6 yd (17 m)

C: 17.5 yd (16 m)

D: 3.9 yd (3.5 m)

Diagonals Baby Blanket

This easy pattern provides lots of opportunities for experimenting with color and layout. The stitches are close fitting, so it is a perfect design for babies. The pattern would also look great worked in grayscale for a geometric throw.

Turn the page for the chart and pattern instructions.

KEY

○ ch

• sl st

+ sc

⋋⊬ sc2tog

⋋⊬⋌ sc3tog

◀ begin row or round

Pattern

Foundation row: With color A, ch2.

Row 1: 3sc in 2nd ch from hook, turn. (3 sts)

Row 2: Ch1, 2sc in first st, sc in next st, 2sc in last st, turn. (5 sts)

Row 3: Ch1, 2sc in first st, sc in each st to last st, 2sc in last st, turn. (7 sts)

Rows 4 + 5: Repeat row 3. (11 sts)

Row 6: Ch1, sc in each st to end, turn.

Rows 7 + 8: Repeat row 3. End color A. (15 sts)

Row 9: Join color B and repeat row 3. (17 sts)

Row 10: Repeat row 6.

Rows 11 + 12: Repeat row 3. End color B. Turn. (21 sts)

Row 13: Join color C and repeat row 3. (23 sts)

Row 14: Repeat row 6.

Rows 15–17: Repeat row 3. (29 sts)

Row 18: Repeat row 6. End color C.

Row 19: Join color B and repeat row 3. (31 sts)

Row 20: Ch1, sc2tog, sc in each st to last 2 sts, sc2tog. End color B. Turn. (29 sts)

Row 21: Join color C and repeat row 6.

Rows 22–24: Repeat row 20. (23 sts)

Row 25: Repeat row 6.

Row 26: Repeat row 20. End color C. Turn. (21 sts)

Rows 27 + 28: Join color B and repeat row 20. (17 sts)

Row 29: Repeat row 6.

Row 30: Repeat row 20. End color B. Turn. (15 sts)

Rows 31 + 32: Join color D and repeat row 20. (11 sts)

Row 33: Repeat row 6.

Rows 34–37: Repeat row 20. (3 sts)

Row 38: Ch1, sc3tog. End color D. (1 st)

Rnd 39 (edging): Turn block over and join color B in any corner, ch1, *(sc, hdc, sc) in corner, sc in each of next 19 row ends to next corner; rep from * 3 times more, sl st in first sc made. End color B. (88 sts)

To make baby blanket: Make 36 blocks. Using color B, join the blocks with a crochet seam, matching the colors at the corners to create a diamond pattern. Add Crab edging (page 105).

Chart

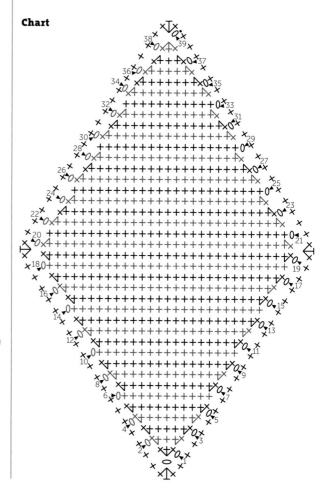

SPECIAL STITCHES

Single crochet 2 together (sc2tog):
Work sc in each of next 2 sts but omit final yo of each sc, yo and pull through all 3 loops on hook.

Single crochet 3 together (sc3tog):
Work sc in each of next 3 sts but omit final yo of each sc, yo and pull through all 4 loops on hook.

This blanket is finished with a simple crab stitch edging, but alternatively you could use Mosaic edging (page 106) for a fuller border, incorporating all the project colors.

- **Hook:** H-8 (5 mm)
- **Yarn:** Light worsted/DK (see page 124 for quantities)
- **Gauge:** 12 sts and 14 rows = 4 in. (10 cm) wide x 6 in. (15 cm) high

A

B

C

D

E

KEY

○ ch

+ sc

‡ Ext sc

⸱ sc in place indicated

† dc

◄ begin row

Coral Shells

This design and color palette is reminiscent of summer vacations at the seaside. Try working in cotton or linen yarn for a beach throw.

Pattern

Foundation row: With color A, ch a multiple of 6 + 5 + 1 turning ch.

Row 1 (RS): Beg in 2nd ch from hook, Ext sc in each ch to end. End color A. Turn.

Row 2 (WS): Join color B, ch1, Ext sc in each st to end. End color B. Turn.

Row 3: Repeat row 2 using color C.

Row 4: Repeat row 2 using color D.

Row 5: Repeat row 2 using color E.

Row 6: Repeat row 2 using color A.

Row 7: Join color B, ch1, sc in first 3 sts, [skip 2 sts, Shell in next st, skip 2 sts, sc in next st] to last 8 sts, skip 2 sts, Shell in next st, skip 2 sts, sc in last 3 sts. End color B. Turn.

Row 8: Join color C, ch3 (counts as 1 dc), dc in next 2 sts, ch5, skip Shell, [(dc, ch1, dc) in next sc, ch5, skip Shell] to last 3 sts, dc in last 3 sts, turn.

Row 9: Ch3 (counts as 1 dc), dc in next st, 4dc in next st, sc in 4th dc of Shell 2 rows below, working over ch5sp of previous row,

[skip 1 st, Shell in ch1sp, skip 1 st, sc in 4th dc of Shell 2 rows below, working over ch5sp of previous row] to last 3 sts, 4dc in next st, dc in last 2 sts. End color C. Turn.

Row 10: Join color D, ch1, sc in first 3 sts, ch2, skip 3 sts, [(dc, ch1, dc) in sc, ch5, skip Shell] to last 7 sts, (dc, ch1, dc) in sc, ch2, skip 3 sts, sc in last 3 sts, turn.

Row 11: Ch1, 1 sc in first 3 sts, [skip 1 st, Shell in ch1sp, sc in 4th dc of Shell 2 rows below, working over ch5sp of previous row] to last 5 sts, skip 1 st, Shell in ch1sp, skip 1 st, sc in last 3 sts. End color D. Turn.

Row 12: Join color E, ch3 (counts as 1 dc), dc in next 2 sts, ch5, skip Shell, [(dc, ch1, dc) in next sc, ch5, skip Shell] to last 3 sts, dc in last 3 sts, turn.

Row 13: Ch3 (counts as 1 dc), dc in next st, 4dc in next st, [sc in 4th dc of Shell 2 rows below, working over ch5sp of previous row, skip 1 st, Shell in ch1sp, skip 1 st] to last ch5sp, sc in 4th dc of Shell 2 rows below, working over ch5sp of previous row, 4dc in next st, dc in last 2 sts. End color E. Turn.

Row 14: Join color A, ch1, sc in first 3 sts, ch2, skip 3 sts, dc in sc, [ch2, skip 3 sts, sc in 4th dc of Shell, ch2, skip 3 sts, dc in sc] to

last 6 sts, ch2, skip 3 sts, sc in last 3 sts, turn.

Row 15: Ch1, Ext sc in first 3 sts, 2Ext sc in ch2sp, [Ext sc in dc, 2Ext sc in ch2sp, Ext sc in sc, 2Ext sc in ch2sp] to last 4 sts and ch2sp, Ext sc in next dc, 2Ext sc in ch2sp, Ext sc in last 3 sts. End color A. Turn.

Repeat rows 2–15 until fabric is the desired length, ending with a row 6.

Chart

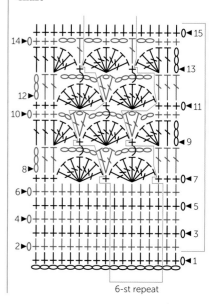

6-st repeat

SPECIAL STITCHES

Extended single crochet (Ext sc):
Insert hook in place indicated and draw up a loop (2 loops on hook), ch1, yo and pull through both loops on hook.

Shell:
Work 7dc in place indicated.

■ **Hook:** H-8 (5 mm)

■ **Yarn:** Light worsted/ DK; quantities below are per block (see also page 124)

■ **Gauge:** Each block = 6 in. (15 cm) square

A: 15.9 yd (14.5 m)

B: 17 yd (15.5 m)

KEY

○ ch

• sl st

+ sc

ૐ BPsc

⊤ hdc

⊤ dc

◀ begin round

Strawberries and Cream

This square begins in the same way as a traditional granny square, but is edged with a shell border. The sample is worked in two colors, but it would look just as good in multiple colors. Try working the first three rounds in bright colors, then work the last four rounds in neutrals.

Pattern

Foundation ring: With color A, ch4, sl st in first ch to form a ring.

Rnd 1: Ch3 (counts as 1 dc), 2dc in ring, [ch2, 3dc in ring] 3 times, ch2, sl st in top of beg ch3. End color A. (12 sts, 4 chsp)

Rnd 2: Join color B in next ch2sp, ch3 (counts as 1 dc), (2dc, ch2, 3dc) in same place, *ch1, (3dc, ch2, 3dc) in ch2sp; rep from * twice more, ch1, sl st in top of beg ch3. End color B. (24 sts, 8 chsp)

Rnd 3: Join color A in next ch2sp, ch3 (counts as 1 dc), (2dc, ch2, 3dc) in same place, *ch1, 3dc in ch1sp, ch1, (3dc, ch2, 3dc) in ch2sp; rep from * twice more, ch1, 3dc in ch1sp, ch1, sl st in top of beg ch3. End color A. (36 sts, 12 chsp)

Rnd 4: Join color B in next ch2sp, ch1, *(sc, ch3, sc) in ch2sp, [sc in next 3 sts, sc in ch1sp] twice, sc in next 3 sts; rep from * 3 times more, sl st in first sc made. End color B. (52 sts, 4 chsp)

Rnd 5: Join color A in next ch3sp, ch3 (counts as 1 dc), 6dc in same place, *skip 2 sts, [sc in next st, skip 1 st, 5dc in next st, skip 1 st] twice, sc in next st, skip 2 sts**, 7dc in ch3sp; rep from * twice more,

then from * to ** once, sl st in top of beg ch3. End color A. (80 sts)

Rnd 6: Join color B in 4th dc of corner shell, ch1, *(sc, ch2, sc) in 4th dc of corner shell, ch3, skip 3 sts, [dc in next sc, ch2, BPsc in 3rd dc of 5dc group, ch2, skip 2 sts] twice, dc in next sc, ch3, skip 3 sts; rep from * 3 times

more, sl st in first sc made. (28 sts, 28 chsp)

Rnd 7: Sl st in corner ch2sp, ch1, *(sc, hdc, sc) in ch2sp, sc in next st, 3sc in ch3sp, [sc in next st, 2sc in ch2sp] 4 times, sc in next st, 3sc in ch3sp, sc in next st; rep from * 3 times more, sl st in first sc made. End color B. (96 sts)

Chart

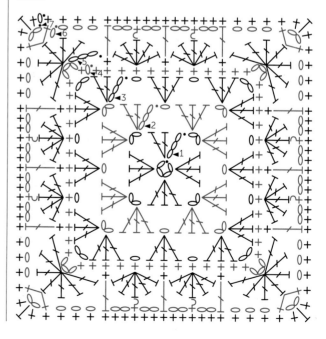

- **Hook:** H-8 (5 mm)
- **Yarn:** Light worsted/ DK; quantities below are per block (see also page 124)
- **Gauge:** Each block = 6 in. (15 cm) square

A: 5.5 yd (5 m)

B: 7.7 yd (7 m)

C: 10.4 yd (9.5 m)

D: 7.7 yd (7 m)

KEY

○ ch

• sl st

+ sc

⊤ hdc

† dc

‡ tr

beg CL

CL

◄ begin round

Fizzy Mint

A fresh, zingy palette makes this square great for summer afghans. It could be worked in cotton or linen yarn for a summer picnic blanket, or try using warm wools and earthy shades for a cozy fireside throw.

Pattern

Foundation ring: With color A, ch5, sl st in first ch to form a ring.

Rnd 1: Beg CL in ring, [ch2, CL in ring] 5 times, ch2, sl st in top of beg CL. End color A. (6 CL, 6 chsp)

Rnd 2: Join color B in ch2sp, ch3 (counts as 1 dc), (dc, ch1, 2dc) in same place, *ch1, (2dc, ch1, 2dc) in next ch2sp; rep from * 4 times more, ch1, sl st in top of beg ch3. End color B. (24 sts, 12 chsp)

Rnd 3: Join color C in next ch1sp, ch1 and sc in same place, [ch2, skip 2 sts, sc in ch1sp] 11 times, ch2, sl st in first sc made. End color C. (12 sts, 12 chsp)

Rnd 4: Join color A in next ch2sp, ch1, [3sc in ch2sp, ch1, skip 1 st] 11 times, 3sc in next ch2sp, ch1, skip 1 st, sl st in first sc made. End color A. (36 sts, 12 chsp)

Rnd 5: Join color C in previous ch1sp, ch1 and sc in same place, [ch3, skip 3 sts, sc in ch1sp] 11 times, ch3, skip 3 sts, sl st in first sc made. End color C. (12 sts, 12 chsp)

Rnd 6: Join color D in next ch3sp, ch3 (counts as 1 dc), 2dc in same place, ch1, *skip 1 st, (3tr, ch2, 3tr) in ch3sp**, [ch1, skip 1 st, 3dc in ch3sp] twice, ch1; rep from * twice more, then from * to ** once, ch1, skip 1 st, 3dc in ch3sp, ch1,

sl st in top of beg ch3. End color D. (48 sts, 16 chsp)

Rnd 7: Join color C in ch2sp, ch1, *(sc, ch3, sc) in ch2sp, [ch3, skip 3 sts, sc in ch1sp] 3 times, ch3, skip 3 sts; rep from * 3 times more, sl st in first sc made. End color C. (20 sts, 20 chsp)

Rnd 8: Join color B in corner ch3sp, ch1, *(sc, hdc, sc) in ch3sp, [ch1, skip 1 st, 3sc in ch3sp]

4 times, ch1; rep from * 3 times more, sl st in first sc made. End color B. (60 sts, 20 chsp)

Rnd 9: Join color C, ch1, sc in first st, [3sc in hdc, sc in each st and ch1sp to next hdc] 3 times, 3sc in hdc, sc in each st and ch1sp to end, sl st in first sc made. End color C. (88 sts)

Sample is shown with Fancy edging (page 106).

Chart

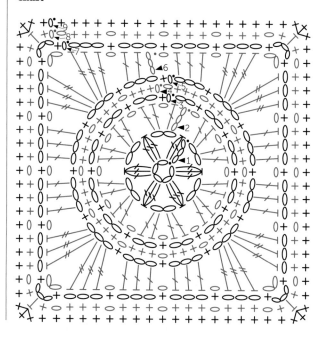

SPECIAL STITCHES

Beginning cluster (beg CL):
Ch3, work 2dc in place indicated
but omit final yo of each dc,
yo and pull through all 3 loops
on hook.

Cluster (CL):
Work 3dc in place indicated but
omit final yo of each dc, yo and
pull through all 4 loops on hook.

- **Hook:** H-8 (5 mm)

- **Yarn:** Light worsted/DK (see page 124 for quantities)

- **Gauge:** 12 sts and 8½ rows = 4 in. (10 cm) square

- **Reversible**

A

B

C

D

E

KEY

○ ch

┬ dc

◄ begin row

Granny Stripes

Everyone loves a granny stripe blanket. The sample uses a set color layout, but you could work the pattern in random colors for a "homey" throw.

Pattern

Foundation row: With color A, ch a multiple of 3 + 2 + 3 turning ch.

Row 1: Beg in 6th ch from hook (first ch3 counts as 1 dc), [3dc in next ch, skip 2 ch] to last 3 ch, 3dc in next ch, skip 1 ch, dc in last ch, turn.

Row 2: Ch3 (counts as 1 dc), dc in same place, skip 3dc, [3dc in gap before next st, skip 3dc] to last st, 2dc in last st. End color A. Turn.

Row 3: Join color B, ch3 (counts as 1 dc), skip 1 st, [3dc in gap before next st, skip 3 sts] to last 2 sts, 3dc in gap before next st, skip 1 st, dc in last st, turn.

Row 4: Ch3 (counts as 1 dc), dc in same place, skip 3 sts, [3dc in gap before next st, skip 3 sts] to last st, 2dc in last st. End color B. Turn.

Rows 5 + 6: Repeat rows 3 + 4 using color C.

Rows 7 + 8: Repeat rows 3 + 4 using color D.

Row 9: Repeat row 3 using color E.

Rows 10 + 11: Repeat row 4 and then row 3 using color D.

Rows 12 + 13: Repeat row 4 and then row 3 using color C.

Rows 14 + 15: Repeat row 4 and then row 3 using color B.

Rows 16–18: Repeat row 4, then row 3, and then row 4 again using color A.

Repeat rows 3–18 until fabric is the desired length.

Chart

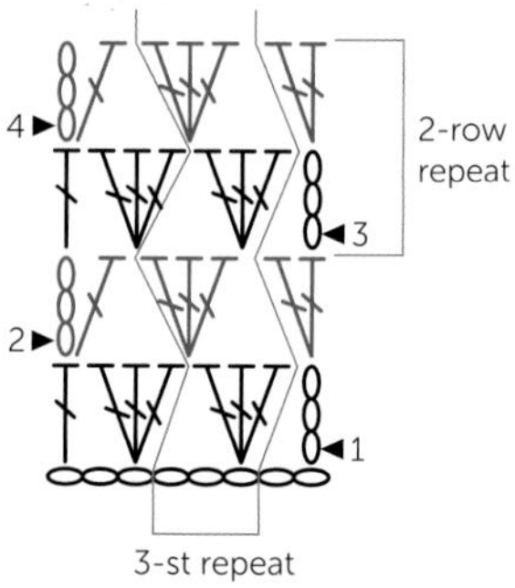

2-row repeat

3-st repeat

- **Hook:** H-8 (5 mm)
- **Yarn:** Light worsted/DK; quantities below are per block (see also page 124)
- **Gauge:** Each block = 6 in. (15 cm) square

A: 1.7 yd (1.5 m)

B: 4.4 yd (4 m)

C: 3.9 yd (3.5 m)

D: 6.1 yd (5.5 m)

E: 7.2 yd (6.5 m)

F: 5 yd (4.5 m)

KEY

○	ch	⚭	beg CL
•	sl st		
+	sc	⚭	CL
T	hdc	‡	W-st
⊤	dc	◄	begin round
⨎	tr		

Lily Pad

The waistcoat stitches on rounds 5 and 6 create the look of knitted stitches, but you could replace these with normal single crochet stitches if you prefer. Join squares together by sewing through the single crochet stitches only, leaving the chain spaces unattached to create an interesting pattern.

Pattern

Foundation ring: With color A, ch4, sl st in first ch to form a ring.

Rnd 1: Ch3 (counts as 1 dc), 11dc in ring, sl st in top of beg ch3. End color A. (12 sts)

Rnd 2: Join color B, beg CL in same place, [ch2, CL in next st] 11 times, ch2, sl st in top of beg CL. End color B. (12 CL, 12 chsp)

Rnd 3: Join color C in ch2sp, ch1, *2sc in ch2sp, ch1, skip CL, 2sc in next ch2sp, skip CL, (2hdc, ch2, 2hdc) in next ch2sp, skip CL; rep from * 3 times more, sl st in first sc made. End color C. (32 sts, 8 chsp)

Rnd 4: Join color D in previous ch2sp, ch3 (counts as 1 dc), (dc, tr, 2dc) in same place, *dc in next 2 sts, ch3, skip 2 sts, sc in ch1sp, ch3, skip 2 sts, dc in next 2 sts**, (2dc, tr, 2dc) in ch2sp; rep from * twice more, then from * to ** once, sl st in top of beg ch3. End color D. (40 sts, 8 chsp)

Rnd 5: Join color E in next tr, ch3 (counts as 1 dc), (dc, tr, 2dc) in same place, *dc in next 4 sts, ch3, W-st in next st, ch3, dc in next 4 sts**, (2dc, tr, 2dc) in tr; rep from * twice more, then from * to ** once, sl st in top of

beg ch3. End color E. (56 sts, 8 chsp)

Rnd 6: Join color F in next tr, ch1, *(sc, hdc, sc) in tr, sc in next 6 sts, ch3, W-st in next st, ch3, sc in next 6 sts; rep from * 3 times more, sl st in first sc made. End color F. (64 sts, 8 chsp)

Chart

SPECIAL STITCHES

Beginning cluster (beg CL):
Ch3, work 2dc in place indicated but omit final yo of each dc, yo, pull through all 3 loops on hook.

Cluster (CL):
Work 3dc in place indicated but omit final yo of each dc, yo and pull through all 4 loops on hook.

Waistcoat stitch (W-st):
Insert hook between vertical V-shaped strands at front of indicated st and work sc.

- **Hook:** H-8 (5 mm)
- **Yarn:** Light worsted/ DK; quantities below are per block (see also page 124)
- **Gauge:** Each block = 6 in. (15 cm) square

A: 9.9 yd (9 m)

B: 2.8 yd (2.5 m)

C: 5 yd (4.5 m)

D: 6.6 yd (6 m)

E: 8.3 yd (7.5 m)

KEY

o ch

• sl st

+ sc

T hdc

◄ begin round

Luxor

This simple block is quick and easy to make. Try working the half double crochet rounds in colors to match your decor, and the single crochet rounds in a neutral color. Staggering where new colors are joined keeps this block from twisting out of shape, which is also a good tip for traditional granny squares.

Chart

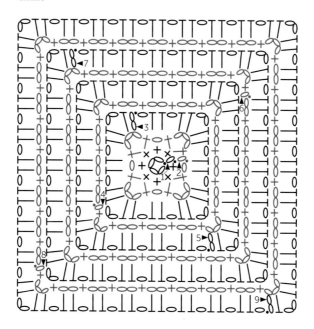

Pattern

Foundation ring: With color A, ch4, sl st in first ch to form a ring.

Rnd 1: Ch1, 8sc in ring, sl st in first sc made. (8 sts)

Rnd 2: Ch1, (sc, ch3, sc) in same place, *ch1, skip 1 st, (sc, ch3, sc) in next st; rep from * twice more, ch1, skip 1 st, sl st in first sc made. End color A. (8 sts, 4 chsp)

Rnd 3: Join color B in next ch3sp, ch2 (counts as 1 hdc), (hdc, ch2, 2hdc) in same place, *ch1, 2hdc in ch1sp, ch1, (2hdc, ch2, 2hdc) in ch3sp; rep from * twice more, ch1, 2hdc in ch1sp, ch1, sl st in top of beg ch2. End color B. (24 sts, 12 chsp)

Rnd 4: Join color A in next ch2sp, ch1, *(sc, ch3, sc) in ch2sp, [ch2, skip 2 sts, sc in ch1sp] twice, ch2; rep from * 3 times more, sl st in first sc made. End color A. (16 sts, 16 chsp)

Rnd 5: Join color C in next ch3sp, ch2 (counts as 1 hdc), (hdc, ch2, 2hdc) in same place, *[ch1, 2hdc in next ch2sp] 3 times, ch1**, (2hdc, ch2, 2hdc) in ch3sp; rep from * twice more, then from * to ** once, sl st in top of beg ch2. End color C. (40 sts, 20 chsp)

Rnd 6: Join color A in next ch2sp, ch1, *(sc, ch3, sc) in ch2sp, [ch2, skip 2 sts, sc in next ch1sp] 4 times, ch2; rep from * 3 times more, sl st in first sc made. End color A. (24 sts, 24 chsp)

Rnd 7: Join color D in next ch3sp, ch2 (counts as 1 hdc), (hdc, ch2, 2hdc) in same place, *[ch1, 2hdc in next ch2sp] 5 times, ch1**, (2hdc, ch2, 2hdc) in ch3sp; rep from * twice more, then from * to ** once, sl st in top of beg ch2. End color D. (56 sts, 28 chsp)

Rnd 8: Join color A in next ch2sp, ch1, *(sc, ch3, sc) in ch2sp, [ch2, skip 2 sts, sc in next ch1sp] 6 times, ch2; rep from * 3 times more, sl st in first sc made. End color A. (32 sts, 32 chsp)

Rnd 9: Join color E in next ch3sp, ch2 (counts as 1 hdc), (hdc, ch2, 2hdc) in same place, *[ch1, 2hdc in next ch2sp] 7 times, ch1**, (2hdc, ch2, 2hdc) in ch3sp; rep from * twice more, then from * to ** once, sl st in top of beg ch2. End color E. (72 sts, 36 chsp)

- **Hook:** H-8 (5 mm)
- **Yarn:** Light worsted/ DK; quantities below are per block (see also page 124)
- **Gauge:** Each block = 6 in. (15 cm) square

A: 1.7 yd (1.5 m)

B: 2.8 yd (2.5 m)

C: 4.4 yd (4 m)

D: 6.6 yd (6 m)

E: 13.7 yd (12.5 m)

KEY

○ ch

• sl st

+ sc

⊤ dc

⊥ tr

◄ begin round

Phoenix

Phoenix is a very easy "circle in a square" pattern. For a colorful afghan, try making the square using random, bright colors for the first three rounds and set colors for the last three rounds.

Pattern

Foundation ring: With color A, ch4, sl st in first ch to form a ring.

Rnd 1: Ch3 (counts as 1 dc), 11dc in ring, sl st in top of beg ch3. End color A. (12 sts)

Rnd 2: Join color B, ch3 (counts as 1 dc), 2dc in same place, [ch1, skip 1 st, 3dc in next st] 5 times, ch1, sl st in top of beg ch3. End color B. (18 sts, 6 chsp)

Rnd 3: Join color C in next ch1sp, ch3 (counts as 1 dc), 2dc in same place, [skip 1 st, 3dc in next st, skip 1 st, 3dc in next ch1sp] 5 times, skip 1 st, 3dc in next st, sl st in top of beg ch3. End color C. (36 sts)

Rnd 4: Join color D in next st, ch3 (counts as 1 dc), 2dc in same place, ch1, skip 2 sts, *(2tr, ch2, 2tr) in next st**, [ch1, skip 2 sts, 3dc in next st] twice, ch1, skip 2 sts; rep from * twice more, then from * to ** once, ch1, skip 2 sts, 3dc in next st, ch1, sl st in top of beg ch3. End color D. (40 sts, 16 chsp)

Rnd 5: Join color E in ch2sp, ch3 (counts as 1 dc), (dc, ch2, 2dc) in same place, *dc in each st and ch1sp to next ch2sp, (2dc, ch2, 2dc) in ch2sp; rep from * twice more, dc in each st and ch1sp to

end, sl st in top of beg ch3. (68 sts, 4 chsp)

Rnd 6: Ch1 and sc in same place, sc in next st, [3sc in ch2sp, sc in each st to next ch2sp] 3 times, 3sc in ch2sp, sc in each st to end, sl st in first sc made. End color E. (80 sts)

Chart

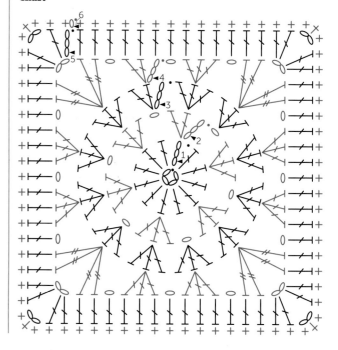

- **Hook:** H-8 (5 mm)
- **Yarn:** Light worsted/DK; quantities below are per block (see also page 124)
- **Gauge:** Each block = 6 x 12 in. (15 x 30 cm)
- **Afghan size:** 42 x 60 in. (105 x 150 cm); 35 blocks joined in 5 rows of 7 blocks

A: 5.5 yd (5 m)

B: 9.9 yd (9 m)

C: 12.1 yd (11 m)

D: 13.2 yd (12 m)

E: 14.8 yd (13.5 m)

F: 15.9 yd (14.5 m)

Granny Quilt

The traditional granny square is an all-time favorite with crocheters. This design starts with a granny square, and then rows of single crochet are worked along one edge to make a rectangle. Try working the single crochet rows all in one color for a patchwork effect. This afghan is finished with a single crochet edging, but the Granny edging on page 109 would also be a great choice.

Turn the page for the chart and pattern instructions.

KEY

- **o** ch
- **•** sl st
- **+** sc
- **ꝓ** dc
- **◄** begin round or row

Pattern

Foundation ring: With color A, ch4, sl st in first ch to form a ring.

Rnd 1: Ch3 (counts as 1 dc), 2dc in ring, [ch2, dc in ring] 3 times, ch2, sl st in top of beg ch3. End color A. (12 sts)

Rnd 2: Join color B in ch2sp, ch3 (counts as 1 dc), 2dc in same place, [ch1, (3dc, ch2, 3dc) in next ch2sp] 3 times, ch1, 3dc in next ch2sp, ch2, sl st in top of beg ch3. End color B. (24 sts)

Rnd 3: Join color C in ch2sp, ch3 (counts as 1 dc), 2dc in same place, *ch1, 3dc in next ch1sp, ch1**, (3dc, ch2, 3 dc) in ch2sp; rep from * twice more, then from * to ** once, 3dc in next ch2sp, ch2, sl st in top of beg ch3. End color C. (36 sts)

Rnd 4: Join color D in ch2sp, ch3 (counts as 1 dc), 2dc in same place, *[ch1, 3dc in next ch1sp] twice, ch1**, (3dc, ch2, 3 dc) in ch2sp; rep from * twice more, then from * to ** once, 3dc in next ch2sp, ch2, sl st in top of beg ch3. End color D. (48 sts)

Rnd 5: Join color E in ch2sp, ch3 (counts as 1 dc), 2dc in same place, *[ch1, 3dc in next ch1sp] 3 times, ch1**, (3dc, ch2, 3dc) in ch2sp; rep from * twice more, then from * to ** once, 3dc in next ch2sp, ch2, sl st in top of beg ch3. End color E. (60 sts)

Rnd 6: Join color F in ch2sp, ch3 (counts as 1 dc), 2dc in same place, *[ch1, 3dc in next ch1sp] 4 times, ch1**, (3dc, ch2, 3dc) in ch2sp; rep from * twice more, then from * to ** once, 3dc in next ch2sp, ch2, sl st in top of beg ch3. End color F. (72 sts)

Row 7: Join color B, ch1 and sc in same place, sc in each st and ch to next corner ch2sp, sc in ch2sp, turn. (25 sts)

Row 8: Ch 1, sc in each st to end. End color B. Turn.

Rows 9 + 10: Repeat row 8 using color C.

Rows 11 + 12: Repeat row 8 using color D.

Rows 13 + 14: Repeat row 8 using color E.

Rows 15 + 16: Repeat row 8 using color F.

Rows 17 + 18: Repeat row 8 using color A.

Rows 19 + 20: Repeat row 8 using color F.

Rows 21 + 22: Repeat row 8 using color E.

Rows 23 + 24: Repeat row 8 using color D.

Rows 25 + 26: Repeat row 8 using color C.

Rows 27 + 28: Repeat row 8 using color B.

To make throw: Make 35 blocks and sew together in 5 rows of 7 blocks, alternating direction of rectangles.

Edging: With color F, work sc in each st and row end along each side and 3sc in each corner.

Chart

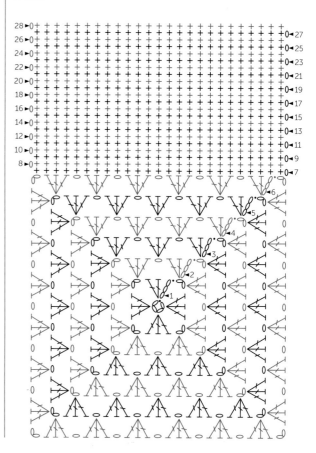

Try working a couple of the single crochet rows in a fluffy yarn for some added interest. Although novelty yarns are trickier to work with, this pattern is a great opportunity for a little experimentation.

- **Hook:** H-8 (5 mm)

- **Yarn:** Light worsted/DK (see page 124 for quantities)

- **Gauge:** Approx. 14½ sts and 16 rows in sc = 4 in. (10 cm) square

- **Reversible**

A

B

C

D

E

F

KEY

o ch

+ sc

) sc in place indicated

◄ begin row

Purpilicious

This lovely open design looks the same on both sides and is quick to work up. Try using just two colors for a bold and striking throw.

Pattern

Foundation row: With color A, ch a multiple of 5 + 3 + 1 turning ch.

Row 1: Beg in 2nd ch from hook, sc in each ch to end, turn.

Row 2: Ch1, sc in each st to end, turn.

Row 3: Ch1, sc in first st, [sc in next st, ch4, skip 4 sts] to last 2 sts, sc in last 2 sts. End color A. Turn.

Row 4: Join color B, ch1, sc in first st, ch1, skip 1 st, [4sc in ch4sp, ch1, skip 1 st] to last st, sc in last st, turn.

Row 5: Ch1, sc in first st, [ch1, skip ch1sp, sc in next 4 sts] to last ch1sp and last st, ch1, skip ch1sp, sc in last st. End color B. Turn.

Row 6: Join color A, ch1, sc in first st, sc in skipped st 3 rows below, working around ch of previous 2 rows, [ch4, skip 4 sts, sc in skipped st 3 rows below, working around ch of previous 2 rows] to last st, sc in last st, turn.

Row 7: Ch1, sc in first st, [sc in next st, 4sc in ch4sp] to last 2 sts, sc in last 2 sts, turn.

Rows 8 + 9: Repeat rows 2 + 3. End color A. Turn.

Rows 10 + 11: Repeat rows 4 + 5 using color C.

Rows 12–15: Repeat rows 6–9 using color A.

Repeat rows 10–15, changing color used for rows 10 + 11 as follows: color D, color E, color F.

Continue repeating rows 10–15 in established color sequence until fabric is the desired length. End with a row 14 (2 rows of sc in colour A).

Chart

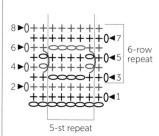

- **Hook:** H-8 (5 mm)

- **Yarn:** Light worsted/ DK (see page 124 for quantities)

- **Gauge:** 16 sts and 14 rows = 4 in. (10 cm) square

A

B

C

D

KEY

o   ch

+   sc

(sc in place indicated

T   hdc

🔵   bobble

◄   begin row

Bobble Band

Bands of single crochet and tactile bobble stitches lie on a bed of half double crochet in this design. The pattern is easy to remember and works up quickly. Use colors to match your decor, or go crazy with color and work the bands in different colorways on a neutral background.

Pattern

Foundation row: With color A, ch a multiple of 4 + 3 + 2 turning ch.

Row 1 (RS): Beg in 4th ch from hook (first ch2 counts as 1 hdc), hdc in each ch to end, turn.

Row 2 (WS): Ch2 (counts as 1 hdc), hdc in each st to end, turn.

Rows 3–5: Repeat row 2. End color A.

Row 6: Join color B, ch1, sc in each st to end. End color B. Turn.

Row 7: Repeat row 6 using color C.

Row 8: Repeat row 6 using color D.

Row 9: Repeat row 6 using color A.

Row 10: Join color C, ch1, sc in first 2 sts, [ch1, skip 1 st, BO in next st, ch1, skip 1 st, sc in next st] to last st, sc in last st. End color C. Turn.

Row 11: Join color A, ch1, sc in first st, [sc in next st, sc in next skipped st 2 rows below, sc in BO, sc in next skipped st 2 rows below]

to last 2 sts, sc in last 2 sts. End color A. Turn.

Row 12: Repeat row 6 using color D.

Row 13: Repeat row 6 using color C.

Row 14: Repeat row 6 using color B.

Row 15: Repeat row 2 using color A.

Repeat rows 2–15 until fabric is the desired length. End with a row 5 (5 rows of hdc in color A).

Chart

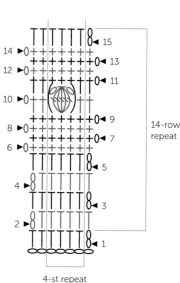

14-row repeat

4-st repeat

SPECIAL STITCH

Bobble (BO):
Work 5dc in place indicated but omit final yo of each dc, yo and pull through all 6 loops on hook.

- **Hook:** H-8 (5 mm)

- **Yarn:** Light worsted/
DK (see page 124
for quantities)

- **Gauge:** Approx.
13½ sts and 10 rows =
4 in. (10 cm) square

A

B

C

D

KEY

o   ch

+   sc

T   hdc

 bobble

◄   begin row

Bibbledy Bobbledy Blue

Comprised mainly of half double crochet stitches, this design works up quite quickly. Rows of single crochet stitches and tactile bobble stitches add some color. Try working each band of single crochet and bobble stitches in a different colorway each time you repeat it.

Pattern

Foundation row: With color A, ch a multiple of 4 + 3 + 2 turning ch.

Row 1 (RS): Beg in 4th ch from hook (first ch2 counts as 1 hdc), hdc in each ch to end, turn.

Row 2 (WS): Ch2 (count as 1 hdc), hdc in each st to end, turn.

Rows 3–5: Repeat row 2. End color A.

Row 6: Join color B, ch1, sc in each st to end. End color B. Turn.

Row 7: Repeat row 6 using color C.

Row 8: Join color D, ch1 and sc in first st, [sc in next st, ch1, skip 1 st, BO in next st, ch1, skip 1 st] to last 2 sts, sc in last 2 sts. End color D. Turn.

Row 9: Join color C, ch1, sc in first 2 sts, [sc in skipped st 2 rows below, sc in BO, sc in skipped st 2 rows below, sc in next st] to last st, sc in last st. End color C. Turn.

Row 10: Repeat row 6 using color B.

Rows 11–15: Repeat row 2 using color A. End color A.

Row 16: Repeat row 6 using color C.

Row 17: Repeat row 2 using color D. End color D.

Row 18: Repeat row 6 using color C.

Row 19: Repeat row 2 using color A.

Repeat rows 2–19 until fabric is the desired length.

Sample is shown with Flounce edging (page 107)

SPECIAL STITCH

Bobble (BO):
Work 5dc in place indicated but omit final yo of each dc, yo and pull through all 6 loops on hook.

Chart

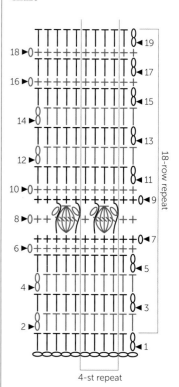

- **Hook:** H-8 (5 mm)

- **Yarn:** Light worsted/ DK (see page 124 for quantities)

- **Gauge:** 10 sts and 12½ rows = 4 in. (10 cm) square

- **Reversible**

A

B

C

D

E

KEY

○ ch

+ sc

↑ dc

✕ X-st

◄ begin row

Crossed Hatch

This easy, lacy pattern works up quickly and is a great way to use up scraps of different colored yarns for a really colorful blanket. Or try alternating two rows worked in a plain color with two rows worked in variegated or self-striping yarn.

Pattern

Foundation row: With color A, ch a multiple of 2 + 2 + 1 turning ch.

Row 1: Beg in 2nd ch from hook, sc in each ch to end, turn.

Row 2: Ch3 (counts as 1 dc), [X-st in next 2 sts] to last st, dc in last st, turn.

Row 3: Ch1, sc in each st to end. End color A. Turn.

Row 4: Join color B, ch1, sc in each st to end, turn.

Row 5: Ch3 (counts as 1 dc), [X-st in next 2 sts] to last st, dc in last st, turn.

Row 6: Ch1, sc in each st to end. End color B. Turn.

Rows 7–9: Repeat rows 4–6 using color C.

Rows 10–12: Repeat rows 4–6 using color D.

Rows 13–15: Repeat rows 4–6 using color E.

Rows 16–18: Repeat rows 4–6 using color A.

Repeat rows 4–18 until fabric is the desired length.

Chart

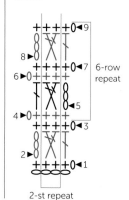

6-row repeat

2-st repeat

SPECIAL STITCH

Cross stitch (X-st): Skip 1 st, dc in next st, dc in skipped st.

- **Hook:** H-8 (5 mm)

- **Yarn:** Light worsted/ DK; quantities below are per block (see also page 124)

- **Gauge:** Each block = 6 in. (15 cm) square

A: 4.4 yd (4 m)

B: 6.6 yd (6 m)

C: 6.6 yd (6 m)

D: 6.6 yd (6 m)

E: 6.6 yd (6 m)

F: 21.9 yd (20 m)

KEY

○ ch

• sl st

+ sc

⊥ Ext sc

T hdc

⊤ dc

‡ tr

⊕ popcorn

◀ begin round

Flower Patch

This block is comprised of four little squares that are sewn together. Each little square could also be used to edge a blanket. Try working each square with a different background color for a patchwork effect.

Pattern

For each block make 4 squares—1 each using colors B, C, D, and E for round 2.

Foundation ring: With color A, ch4, sl st in first ch to form a ring.

Rnd 1: Ch1, 8Ext sc in ring, sl st in first Ext sc made. End color A. (8 sts)

Rnd 2: Join color B, C, D, or E, *(ch3, PC) in same place, ch3, sl st in next st; rep from * 7 times more, working last sl st in base of first PC made. End color. (8 PC)

Rnd 3: Join color F in top of PC, ch1 and sc in same place, *(ch3, sc in top of next PC, ch4**, sc in top of next PC; rep from * twice more, then from * to ** once, sl st in first sc made. (8 sts, 8 chsp)

Rnd 4: Ch2 (counts as 1 hdc), *3sc in ch3sp, hdc in next st, (hdc, dc, tr, dc, hdc) in ch4sp**, hdc in next

Chart

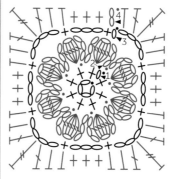

st; rep from * twice more, then from * to ** once, sl st in top of beg ch2. End color F. (40 sts)

Join squares together by sewing through back loops of sts using color F.

Sample is shown with Prism edging (page 109).

SPECIAL STITCHES

Extended single crochet (Ext sc):
Insert hook in place indicated and draw up a loop (2 loops on hook), ch1, yo and pull through both loops on hook.

Popcorn (PC):
Work 5dc in place indicated, remove hook from loop, insert hook from front to back in top of first dc, pick up dropped loop and pull through loop on hook.

- **Hook:** H-8 (5 mm)

- **Yarn:** Light worsted/DK; quantities below are per block (see also page 124)

- **Gauge:** Each block = 6 in. (15 cm) square

A: 6.6 yd (6 m)

B: 6.6 yd (6 m)

C: 6.6 yd (6 m)

D: 9.3 yd (8.5 m)

E: 18.1 yd (16.5 m)

KEY

ℓ magic ring

○ ch

• sl st

+ sc

ϟ BPsc

T hdc

Ŧ dc

Ⱶ W-st

◄ begin round

Folk Flower

Inspired by folk art, this little flower block is tactile and bright. The waistcoat stitches on the last round are easy to do and create the look of knitted stitches, but you could replace these with normal single crochet stitches if you prefer.

Pattern

Foundation ring: With color A, make a magic ring.

Rnd 1: Ch1, 8sc in ring, sl st in first sc made. End color A. (8 sts)

Rnd 2: Join color B, ch1, 2sc in each st around, sl st in first sc made. End color B. (16 sts)

Rnd 3: Join color C, ch1, 2sc in each st around, sl st in first sc made. End color C. (32 sts)

Rnd 4: Join color D, ch3 (counts as 1 dc), dc in same place, ch3, sl st in next st, [sl st in next st, ch3, 2dc in each of next 2 sts, ch3, sl st in next st] 7 times, sl st in next st, ch3, 2dc in next st, sl st in top of beg ch3. End color D. (8 petals)

Rnd 5: Join color E in next sl st between petals, ch3 (counts as 1 dc), *BPsc in next 4 sts, (dc, ch2, dc) in sl st between petals, BPsc in next 4 sts**, dc in sl st between petals; rep from * twice more, then from * to ** once, sl st in top of beg ch3. (44 sts, 4 chsp)

Rnd 6: Ch3 (counts as 1 dc), dc in next 5 sts, *(2dc, ch2, 2dc) in ch2sp**, dc in next 11 sts; rep from * twice more, then from * to ** once, dc in next 5 sts, sl st in top of beg ch3. End color E. (60 sts, 4 chsp)

Rnd 7: Join color A in corner ch2sp, ch1, *(sc, hdc, sc) in ch2sp, BPsc in next 15 sts; rep from * 3 times more, sl st in first sc made. End color A. (72 sts)

Chart

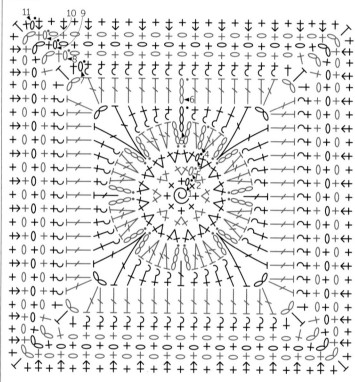

Rnd 8: Join color D in corner hdc, ch1, *(sc, ch2, sc) in hdc, [ch1, skip 1 st, sc in next st] 8 times, ch1, skip 1 st; rep from * 3 times more, sl st in first sc made. End color D. (40 sts, 40 chsp)

Rnd 9: Join color C in corner ch2sp, ch1, *(sc, ch2, sc) in ch2sp, [ch1, skip 1 st, sc in next ch1sp] 9 times, ch1, skip 1 st; rep from * 3 times more, sl st in first sc made. End color C. (44 sts, 44 chsp)

Rnd 10: Join color B in corner ch2sp, ch1, *(sc, ch2, sc) in ch2sp, [ch1, skip 1 st, sc in next st] 10 times, ch1, skip 1 st; rep from * 3 times more, sl st in first sc made. End color B. (48 sts, 48 chsp)

Rnd 11: Join color E in ch2sp, ch1, *(sc, hdc, sc) in ch2sp, W-st in each st and sc in each ch1sp to next corner ch2sp; rep from * 3 times more, sl st in first sc made. End color E. (104 sts)

SPECIAL STITCH

Insert hook between vertical V-shaped strands at front of indicated st and work sc.

- **Hook:** H-8 (5 mm)
- **Yarn:** Light worsted/DK; quantities below are per block (see also page 124)
- **Gauge:** Each block = 6 in. (15 cm) square

A: 2.8 yd (2.5 m)

B: 6.6 yd (6 m)

C: 7.2 yd (6.5 m)

D: 5.5 yd (5 m)

E: 7.7 yd (7 m)

KEY

○ ch
• sl st
+ sc
T hdc
⊤ dc
⊤ tr
⋀ sc3tog
⋀ dc2tog
◄ begin round

Knotty but Nice

Reminiscent of Celtic knotwork designs, this block has a striking geometric look. Try working in black, white, and grays for a bold throw. If your chain stitches are too loose or too tight, round 2 may cause puckering, so feel free to increase or decrease the number of chains if necessary.

Pattern

Foundation ring: With color A, ch4, sl st in first ch to form a ring.

Rnd 1: Ch3 (counts as 1 dc), 2dc in ring, [ch10, 3dc in ring] 3 times, ch10, sl st in top of beg ch3. End color A. (12 sts, 4 chsps)

Rnd 2: Join color B in ch10sp, ch3 (counts as 1 dc), (5dc, ch2, 6dc) in same place, *sc3tog in next 3 sts, (6dc, ch2, 6dc) in next ch10sp; rep from * twice more, sc3tog in next 3 sts, sl st in top of beg ch3. End color B. (52 sts, 4 chsps)

Rnd 3: Join color C in ch2sp, ch3 (counts as 1 dc), (2dc, ch2, 3dc) in same place, *dc in next 4 sts, skip 2 sts, tr in sc3tog, skip 2 sts, dc in next 4 sts**, (3dc, ch2, 3dc) in ch2sp; rep from * twice more, then from * to ** once, sl st in top of beg ch3. End color C. (60 sts, 4 chsps)

Rnd 4: Join color D in ch2sp, ch1, *(sc, hdc, sc) in ch2sp, sc in next 3 sts, hdc in next 3 sts, dc2tog, hdc in next 3 sts, sc in next 3 sts; rep from * 3 times more, sl st in first sc made. End color D. (64 sts)

Rnd 5: Join color E in corner hdc, ch2 (counts as 1 hdc), (dc, hdc) in same place, *hdc in each st to next corner hdc, (hdc, dc, hdc) in corner hdc; rep from * twice more, hdc in each st to end, sl st in top of beg ch2. End color E. (72 sts)

Chart

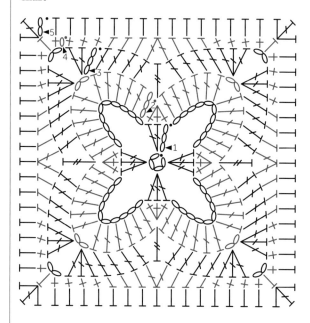

SPECIAL STITCHES

Single crochet 3 together (sc3tog):
Work sc in each of next 3 sts but omit final yo of each sc, yo and pull through all 4 loops on hook.

Double crochet 2 together (dc2tog):
Work dc in next dc but omit final yo, skip tr, work another incomplete dc in next dc, yo and pull through all 3 loops on hook.

Skill level: 3

- **Hook:** H-8 (5 mm)

- **Yarn:** Light worsted/ DK; quantities below are per block (see also page 124)

- **Gauge:** Each block = 6 in. (15 cm) square

- **Afghan size:** 36 in. (90 cm) square; 36 blocks joined in 6 rows of 6 blocks

A: 3.3 yd (3 m)

B: 6.6 yd (6 m)

C: 18.6 yd (17 m)

D: 7.2 yd (6.5 m)

E: 7.2 yd (6.5 m)

F: 7.2 yd (6.5 m)

G: 7.2 yd (6.5 m)

Roisin Baby Blanket

Using the traditional Irish rose as a starting point, this block is packed with tactile loveliness, and the 3D flowers make the finished blanket deliciously chunky. You can work the petal rounds all in one color or even try different colors for each block.

Turn the page for the chart and pattern instructions.

Chart

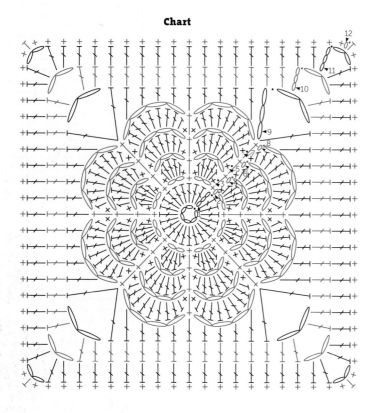

KEY

○	ch
•	sl st
+	sc
⊤	hdc
⊥	dc
◄	begin round

Pattern

Foundation ring: With color A, ch6, sl st in first ch to form a ring.

Rnd 1: Ch3 (counts as 1 dc), 23dc in ring, sl st in top of beg ch3. End color A. (24 sts)

Rnd 2: Join color B, ch1 and sc in same place, [ch2, skip 2 sts, sc in next st] 7 times, ch2, skip 2 sts, sl st in first sc made. (8 sts)

Rnd 3: [(Sc, hdc, 3dc, hdc, sc) in ch2sp] 8 times, sl st in first sc made. End color B. (56 sts)

Rnd 4: Fold petals of last round forward and work into sts of round 2: join color C in sc on round 2, ch1 and sc in same place, [ch3, sc in next sc] 7 times, ch3, sl st in first sc made. (8 sts)

Rnd 5: [(Sc, hdc, 5dc, hdc, sc) in ch3sp] 8 times, sl st in first sc made. (72 sts)

Rnd 6: Fold petals of last round forward and work into sts of round 4: [sc in next sc, ch4] 8 times, sl st in first sc made. (8 sts)

Rnd 7: [(Sc, hdc, 7dc, hdc, sc) in ch4sp] 8 times, sl st in first sc made. End color C. (88 sts)

Rnd 8: Fold petals of last round forward and work into sts of round 6: join color D in sc on round 6, ch1 and sc in same place, [ch4, sc in next sc] 7 times, ch4, sl st in first sc made. (8 sts)

Rnd 9: Ch3 (counts as 1 dc), *4dc in ch4sp, dc in next sc, 4dc in ch4sp**, (dc, ch2, dc) in next st; rep from * twice more, then from * to ** once, dc in first st, ch2, sl st in top of beg ch3. (44 sts)

Rnd 10: Ch3 (counts as 1 dc), dc in same place, [dc in each st to next corner ch2sp, (2dc, ch2, 2dc) in ch2sp] 3 times, dc in each st to first corner ch2sp, 2dc in ch2sp, ch2, sl st in top of beg ch3. (60 sts)

Rnd 11: Repeat round 10. (76 sts)

Rnd 12: Ch1, sc in same place, [sc in each st to next corner ch2sp, (sc, hdc, sc) in ch2sp] 3 times, sc in each st to first corner ch2sp, (sc, hdc) in ch2sp, sl st in first sc made. End color D. (88 sts)

To make baby blanket: Make 36 blocks, working 9 blocks each using colors D, E, F, and G for rounds 8–12. Join with a crochet seam, arranging the blocks in any color order you wish. Add Curvy edging (page 104).

The 3D flowers make this a thick and cozy blanket. For a more delicate afghan, try working in a lighter weight yarn, but remember that yarn quantities will be different if you do so.

- **Hook:** H-8 (5 mm)
- **Yarn:** Light worsted/ DK (see page 124 for quantities)
- **Gauge:** 14 sts and 5¾ rows = 4 in. (10 cm) square

A

B

C

D

E

F

KEY

○	ch	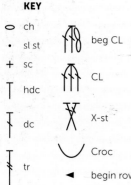 beg CL	
•	sl st		
+	sc	CL	
⊤	hdc	X-st	
⊤	dc	Croc	
⊤	tr	◄ begin row	

Pond

This watery design features offset crocodile stitches to create tactile leaves, and cluster stitches to form flower heads. Keep an eye on when to turn the work.

Pattern

Foundation row: With color A, ch a multiple of 7 + 1 + 3 turning ch.

Row 1 (RS): Beg in 5th ch from hook (first ch3 counts as 1 dc), dc in each ch to end, turn.

Row 2 (WS): Ch3 (counts as 1 dc), dc in each st to end, turn.

Row 3: Repeat row 2. End color A.

Row 4: Join color B, ch5 (counts as 1 dc, ch2), skip 3 sts, dc in gap before next st, [ch2, skip 3 sts, 2dc in next st, ch2, skip 3 sts, dc in gap before next st] to last 4 sts, ch2, skip 3 sts, dc in last st, turn.

Row 5: Sl st in first st, ch2, [sl st in next st, Croc over next 2 sts] to last 2 sts, sl st in next st, ch2, sl st in last st. End color B. Turn.

Row 6: Join color C, ch5 (counts as 1 dc, ch2), 2dc in next sl st, ch2, [dc in center of Croc, ch2, 2dc in next sl st, ch2] to last st, dc in last sl st, turn.

Row 7: Sl st in first st, [Croc over next 2 sts, sl st in next st] to end. End color C. Do not turn.

Row 8: Join color D in first sl st of last row, ch1, sc in first sl st, [9dc in center of next Croc, sc in next sl st] to end. End color D. Do not turn.

Row 9: Join color E in first dc of row 8, beg CL, [ch3, CL] twice, ch3, skip 1 st, *[CL, ch3] 3 times, skip 1 st; rep from * to last 10 sts, [CL, ch3] twice, CL, skip last st. End color E. Do not turn.

Row 10: Join color F in first sc of row 8, ch4 (counts as 1 tr), *(hdc, 2sc) in next ch3sp, (2sc, hdc) in next ch3sp, tr in next skipped st on row 8; rep from * to end, turn.

Row 11: Repeat row 2.

Row 12: Ch3 (counts as 1 dc), *[X-st] 3 times, dc in next st; rep from * to end. End color F. Do not turn.

Row 13: Join color A in first st of last row, ch3 (counts as 1 dc), *[X-st] 3 times, dc in next st; rep from * to end, turn.

Rows 14 + 15: Repeat row 2.

Repeat rows 2–15 until fabric is the desired length.

Chart

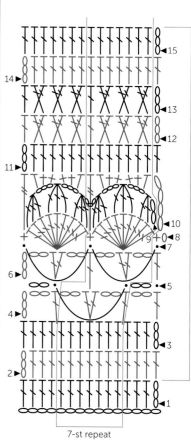

14-row repeat

7-st repeat

SPECIAL STITCHES

Crocodile stitch (Croc):
5dc around next dc, working from top to bottom of post; 5dc around next dc, working from bottom to top of post.

Beginning cluster (beg CL):
Ch2, work dc in each of next 2 sts but omit final yo of each dc, yo and pull through all 3 loops on hook.

Cluster (CL):
Work dc each of next 3 sts but omit final yo of each dc, yo and pull through all 4 loops on hook.

Cross stitch (X-st):
Skip 1 st, dc in next st, dc in skipped st.

- **Hook:** H-8 (5 mm)
- **Yarn:** Light worsted/ DK (see page 124 for quantities)
- **Gauge:** 12 sts and 9½ rows = 4 in. (10 cm) square

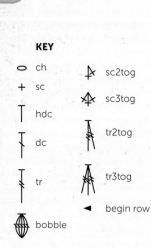

A

B

C

D

E

F

KEY

○	ch	⊀	sc2tog
+	sc	⟨⟩	sc3tog
T	hdc		
⊺	dc	⫫	tr2tog
		⋔	tr3tog
⫯	tr		
◀		begin row
⬯	bobble		

Chutes and Ladders

This bright design is reminiscent of the childhood board game, and would be a great afghan for a toddler. Try working in natural colors for an earthy afghan for the home. Keep an eye on when to turn the work.

Pattern

Foundation row: With color A, ch a multiple of 6 + 1 + 3 turning ch.

Row 1: Beg in 5th ch from hook (first ch3 counts as 1 dc), dc in each ch to end. End color A. Do not turn.

Row 2: Join color B in first st of last row, ch3 (counts as 1 dc), dc in each st to end. End color B. Do not turn.

Row 3: Repeat row 2 using color C. End color C. Turn.

Row 4: Join color D, ch1, sc in first 3 sts, [BO in next st, sc in next 2 sts] to last st, sc in last st. End color D. Turn.

Row 5: Join color C, ch3 (counts as 1 dc), dc in each st to end. End color C. Do not turn.

Row 6: Join color B in first st of last row and repeat row 5. End color B. Do not turn.

Row 7: Join color A in first st of last row and repeat row 5. End color A. Turn.

Row 8: Join color D, ch1, sc in each st to end. End color D. Turn.

Row 9: Join color E, ch1, sc in first st, *hdc in next st, dc in next st, 3dc in next st, dc in next st, hdc in

next st, sc in next st; rep from * to end. End color E. Turn.

Row 10: Join color F, ch1, sc2tog in first 2 sts, *sc in next 2 sts, 3sc in next st, sc in next 2 sts**, sc3tog; rep from * to last 7 sts, rep from * to ** once, sc2tog in last 2 sts. End color F. Turn.

Row 11: Repeat row 10 using color D.

Row 12: Repeat row 10 using color F.

Row 13: Join color E, ch3, tr in next st, *dc in next st, hdc in next st, sc in next st, hdc in next st, dc in next st**, tr3tog; rep from * to last 7 sts, rep from * to ** once, tr2tog in last 2 sts. End color E. Turn.

Row 14: Join color D, ch1, sc in each st to end. End color D. Turn

Row 15: Repeat row 5 using color A.

Repeat rows 2–15 until fabric is the desired length.

Sample is shown with Curvy edging (page 104).

Chart

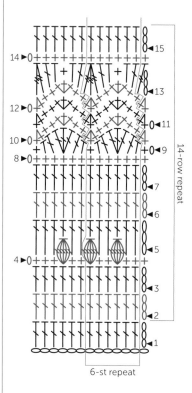

14-row repeat

6-st repeat

SPECIAL STITCHES

Bobble (BO):
Work 5dc in place indicated but omit final yo of each dc, yo and pull through all 6 loops on hook.

Single crochet 2 together (sc2tog):
Work sc in each of next 2 sts but omit final yo of each sc, yo and pull through all 3 loops on hook.

Single crochet 3 together (sc3tog):
Work sc in each of next 3 sts but omit final yo of each sc, yo and pull through all 4 loops on hook.

Treble 2 together (tr2tog):
Work tr in each of next 2 sts but omit final yo of each tr, yo and pull through all 3 loops on hook.

Treble 3 together (tr3tog):
Work tr in each of next 3 sts but omit final yo of each tr, yo and pull through all 4 loops on hook.

- **Hook:** H-8 (5 mm)

- **Yarn:** Light worsted/ DK; quantities below are per block (see also page 124)

- **Gauge:** Each block = 6 in. (15 cm) square

- **Crochet techinique:** Tapestry (page 119)

- **Reversible**

A: 25.2 yd (23 m)

B: 12.1 yd (11 m)

Tile

This simple block uses just two colors. On the middle section of the block, carry the unused color along the wrong side and work single crochet over it. Try laying out squares in opposite directions to create an interesting pattern.

Pattern

Foundation row: With color A, ch22 + 1 turning ch.

Working from chart: Start at the bottom right-hand corner of the chart and work in single crochet, beginning the first row in the 2nd ch from hook. Each square represents 1 stitch. Right-side rows are read from right to left and wrong-side rows are read from left to right. Remember to ch1 at the beginning of each row for a turning ch (this does not count as a stitch).

To change to a different color in the middle of a row: Work to 1 stitch before the color change. Begin this stitch normally, working to the last yarn over, then drop the current color to the wrong side of the work, pick up the new color, and use it to complete the stitch. Hold the unused color along the top edge and work single crochet over it.

Chart

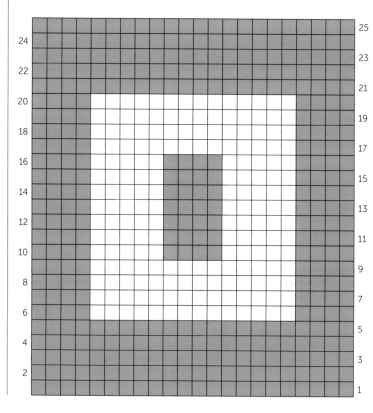

- **Hook:** H-8 (5 mm)

- **Yarn:** Light worsted/ DK; quantities below are per block (see also page 124)

- **Gauge:** Each block = 6 in. (15 cm) square

A: 12.1 yd (11 m)

B: 8.8 yd (8 m)

C: 3.9 yd (3.5 m)

D: 12.1 yd (11 m)

KEY

○ ch

• sl st

+ sc

⊤ hdc

† dc

beg CL

CL

◄ begin round

Tulips

This block starts as a circle of tulips by working V-stitches in green to create sepals and then cluster stitches on the following round to form the flower heads. A square border of tulips finishes the block.

Pattern

Foundation ring: With color A, ch5, sl st in first ch to form a ring.

Rnd 1: Ch1, 16sc in ring, sl st in first sc made. End color A. (16 sts)

Rnd 2: Join color B, ch4 (counts as 1 dc, ch1), dc in same place, [skip 1 st, V-st in next st] 7 times, sl st in 3rd ch of beg ch4. End color B. (16 sts, 8 chsps)

Rnd 3: Join color C in next ch1sp, beg CL in same place, [ch4, skip 2 sts, CL in ch1sp] 7 times, ch4, sl st in top of beg CL. End color C. (8 CL, 8 chsp)

Rnd 4: Join color A in next ch4sp, ch2 (counts as 1 hdc), (hdc, sc, 2hdc) in same place, *(hdc, 2dc, ch2, 2dc, hdc) in next ch4sp**, (2hdc, sc, 2hdc) in next ch4sp; rep from * twice more, then from * to ** once, sl st in top of beg ch2. End color A. (44 sts, 4 chsps)

Rnd 5: Join color B in next corner ch2sp, ch4 (counts as 1 dc, ch1), (dc, ch1, dc) in same place, *[skip 1 st, V-st in next st] 5 times**, ([dc, ch1] twice, dc) in corner ch2sp; rep from * twice more, then from * to ** once, sl st in 3rd ch of beg ch4. End color B. (52 sts, 28 chsps)

Rnd 6: Join color D in next ch1sp, beg CL in same place, *ch5, CL in next ch1sp, [ch2, skip 2 sts, CL in next ch1sp] 6 times; rep from * twice more, ch5, CL in next ch1sp, [ch2, skip 2 sts, CL in next ch1sp] 5 times, sl st in top of beg CL. End color D. (28 CL, 28 chsp)

Rnd 7: Join color A in corner ch5sp, ch1, *(2sc, hdc, 2sc) in ch5sp, [3sc in ch2sp] 6 times; rep from * 3 times more, sl st in first sc made. End color A. (92 sts)

Chart

- **Hook:** H-8 (5 mm)

- **Yarn:** Light worsted/ DK (see page 124 for quantities)

- **Gauge:** 14 sts and 8 rows = 4 in. (10 cm) square

- **Reversible**

A

B

C

D

E

KEY

o   ch

+   sc

⊤   hdc

⊤   dc

⊤   tr

◄   begin row

Wavy

This simple design comprised of straight and wavy rows is a great beginner project. It would look beautiful in all sorts of different colorways.

Pattern

Foundation row: With color A, ch a multiple of 14 + 13 + 3 turning ch.

Row 1: Beg in 5th ch from hook (first ch3 counts as 1 dc), dc in each ch to end, turn.

Row 2: Ch3 (counts as 1 dc), dc in each st to end. End color A. Turn.

Rows 3 + 4: Repeat row 2 using color B.

Rows 5 + 6: Repeat row 2 using color C.

Row 7: Join color D, ch1, sc in first st, *hdc in next 2 sts, dc in next 2 sts, tr in next 3 sts, dc in next 2 sts, hdc in next 2 sts**, sc in next 3 sts; rep from * to last 12 sts, rep from * to ** once, sc in last st. End color D. Turn.

Row 8: Join color E, ch4 (counts as 1 tr), dc in next 2 sts, hdc in next 2 sts, sc in next 3 sts, hdc in next 2 sts, dc in next 2 sts, *tr in next 3 sts, dc in next 2 sts, hdc in next 2 sts, sc in next 3 sts, hdc in next 2 sts, dc in next 2 sts; rep from * to last st, tr in last st. End color E. Turn.

Rows 9–12: Repeat rows 7 + 8 twice more.

Row 13: Join color A, ch3 (counts as 1 dc), dc in each st to end, turn.

Repeat rows 2–13 until fabric is the desired length.

Sample is shown with Mosaic edging (page 106).

Chart

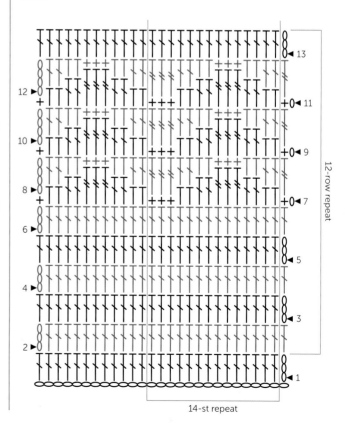

12-row repeat

14-st repeat

- **Hook:** H-8 (5 mm)
- **Yarn:** Light worsted/ DK; quantities below are per block (see also page 124)
- **Gauge:** Each block = 4 in. (10 cm) square
- **Reversible**

A: 10.4 yd (9.5 m)

B: 11 yd (10 m)

C: 3.9 yd (3.5 m)

D: 20.3 yd (18.5 m)

KEY

○ ch

• sl st

+ sc

⊤ hdc

† dc

⌡ BPdc

‡ tr

◄ begin round

Purple Petal Eater

Use bright colors for the flowers and a neutral shade for the background to create a really colorful afghan. You could also try working the flowers in lighter shades on bright backgrounds.

Pattern

Foundation ring: With color A, ch5, sl st in first ch to form a ring.

Rnd 1: Ch1, 16sc in ring, sl st in first sc made. End color A. (16 sts)

Rnd 2: Join color B, ch3 (counts as 1 dc), dc in same place, [2dc in next st] 15 times, sl st in top of beg ch3. End color B. (32 sts)

Rnd 3: Join color A in gap between 2dc, ch1 and sc in same place, [sc in gap before next st] 31 times, sl st in first sc made. End color A. (32 sts)

Rnd 4: Join color C in next st, ch1 and sc in same place, 3dc in next st, sc in next st, [skip 1 st, sc in next st, 3dc in next st, sc in next st] 7 times, skip 1 st, sl st in first sc made. End color C. (40 sts)

Rnd 5: Join color B in next st, ch2 (counts as 1 hdc), dc in same place, 3dc in next st, (dc, hdc) in next st, sc2tog in next 2 sts, *(hdc, dc) in next st, 3dc in next st, (dc, hdc) in next st, sc2tog in next 2 sts; rep from * 6 times more, sl st in top of beg ch2. End color B. (64 sts)

Rnd 6: Join color A, ch1 and sc in same place, 2sc in each of next 5 sts, sc in next st, *BPdc in skipped st on round 3, sc in next st, 2sc in each of next 5 sts, sc in next st; rep from * 6 times more, BPdc in skipped st on round 3, sl st in first sc made. End color A. (104 sts)

Chart

Rnd 7: Fold petals forward and join color D in sc2tog on round 5, ch1 and sc in same place, *ch4, sc in next sc2tog on round 5, ch6**, sc in next sc2tog on round 5; rep from * twice more, then from * to ** once, sl st in first sc made. (8 sts, 8 chsp)

Rnd 8: Ch3 (counts as 1 dc), 3dc in ch4sp, *dc in next st, (4dc, ch2, 4dc) in ch6sp**, dc in next st, 4dc in ch4sp; rep from * twice more, then from * to ** once, sl st in top of beg ch3. (56 sts, 4 chsp)

Rnd 9: Ch3 (counts as 1 dc), *dc in each st to corner ch2sp, (dc, tr, dc) in ch2sp; rep from * 3 times more, dc in each st to end, sl st in top of beg ch3. (68 sts)

Rnd 10: Ch1 and sc in same place, *sc in each st to corner tr, (sc, hdc, sc) in corner tr; rep from * 3 times more, sc in each st to end, sl st in first sc made. End color D. (76 sts)

- **Hook:** H-8 (5 mm)
- **Yarn:** Light worsted/ DK (see page 124 for quantities)
- **Gauge:** Approx. 13½ sts and 6½ rows = 4 in. (10 cm) square

A

B

C

D

E

F

KEY

○ ch

+ sc

† dc

◄ begin row

Sideways

This is a lovely design because there is really only one row of instructions to remember. You could work the pattern in as many or as few colors as you like. The sample changes color every row, but you could also work several rows in each color.

Pattern

Foundation row: With color A, ch a multiple of 4 + 5 + 4 turning ch.

Row 1 (RS): 3dc in 5th ch from hook, skip 3 ch, *(sc, ch3, 3dc) in next ch, skip 3 ch; rep from * to last ch, sc in last ch. End color A. Turn.

Row 2 (WS): Join color B, (ch4, 3dc) in first sc, *(sc, ch3, 3dc) in next ch3sp; rep from * to last ch4sp, sc in last ch4sp. End color B. Turn.

Row 3: Repeat row 2 using color C.

Row 4: Repeat row 2 using color D.

Row 5: Repeat row 2 using color E.

Row 6: Repeat row 2 using color F.

Row 7: Repeat row 2 using color A.

Repeat rows 2–7 until fabric is the desired length.

Last row: Join next color in sequence, (ch4, 2dc) in first sc, *(sc, hdc, dc) in next ch3sp; rep from * to last ch4sp, sc in last ch4sp. End color.

Sample is shown with Spikes edging (page 105).

Chart

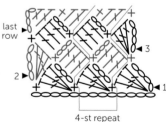

last row

2 ►

◄ 3

◄ 1

4-st repeat

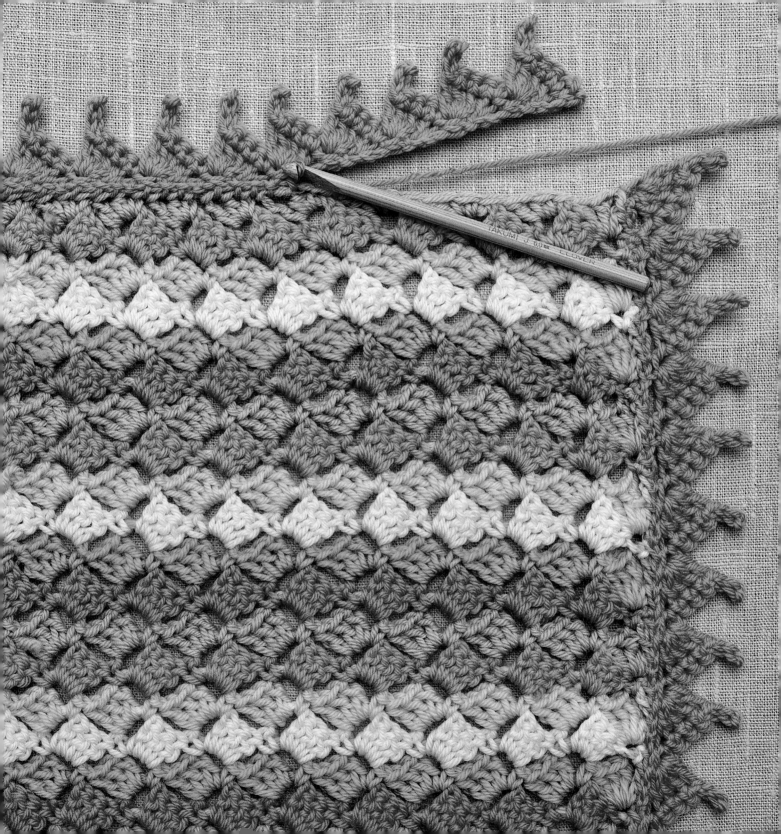

Skill level: 2

- **Hook:** H-8 (5 mm)

- **Yarn:** Light worsted/DK; quantities below are for afghan shown (see also page 124)

- **Gauge:** Approx. 13½ sts and 21 rows = 4 in. (10 cm) square

- **Afghan size:** 60 x 72 in. (150 x 180 cm)

- **Reversible**

A: 788 yd (720 m)

B: 788 yd (720 m)

C: 788 yd (720 m)

D: 788 yd (720 m)

E: 788 yd (720 m)

F: 788 yd (720 m)

G: 788 yd (720 m)

Spiky Waves Throw

This is a simple but effective pattern. The sample shown has been made using a large color palette, but the design would also look great worked in two colors. Take care not to work the spike stitches too tight, but also not too loose.

Turn the page for the chart and pattern instructions.

KEY

○   ch

+   sc

↑   spike sc

◄   begin row

Pattern

Foundation row: With color A, ch a multiple of 10 + 1 + 1 turning ch. To match afghan shown, ch202.

Row 1: Beg in 2nd ch from hook, sc in each ch to end, turn.

Rows 2–6: Ch1, sc in each st to end. End color A. Turn.

Row 7: Join color B, ch1, sc in first st, [spike sc 2 rows below, spike sc 3 rows below, spike sc 4 rows below, spike sc 5 rows below, spike sc 6 rows below, spike sc 5 rows below, spike sc 4 rows below, spike sc 3 rows below, spike sc 2 rows below, sc in next st] to end, turn.

Rows 8–12: Repeat rows 2–6. End color B.

Row 13: Join color C, ch1, sc in first st, [*spike sc 5 rows below, spike sc 4 rows below, spike sc 3 rows below, spike sc 2 rows below, sc in next st, spike sc 2 rows below, spike sc 3 rows below, spike sc 4 rows below, spike sc 5 rows below**, spike sc 6 rows below] to last 10 sts; rep from * to ** once more, sc in last st, turn.

Repeat rows 2–13 until fabric is the desired length, changing color when instructed following the color sequence A–G (42 rows to complete color sequence).

To make the throw: Work 20 repeats across and repeat the color sequence A–G nine times in total.

Chart

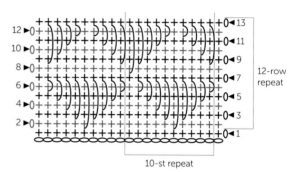

12-row repeat

10-st repeat

SPECIAL STITCH

Spike single crochet (spike sc): Insert hook in next st on specified row below the current row, yo and pull up a loop, lengthen loop to height of working row, yo and pull through both loops on hook.

You can use the same design to make matching pillows for your afghan. Start with a chain multiple that is long enough to cover the width of the pillow form. Work as many rows as needed to cover both front and back of the pillow form, and then sew up the three edges.

Edgings

Every afghan deserves a
beautiful edging, so here are
12 edging patterns for you to
choose from, using both sew-on
and crochet-on methods. Refer to
page 122 for more information
about edging techniques to get
the perfect finish.

Flowery page 107

Flounce page 107

Arches page 105

Spikes page 105

Mosaic page 106

Fancy page 106

Ruffled page 108

Curvy page 104

Crab page 105

Knitty page 104

Granny page 109

Prism page 109

Knitty

A
B
C
Base round

KEY

- ⬭ ch
- • sl st
- + sc
- ‡ W-st
- ◄ begin round

■ **Hook:** H-8 (5 mm)
■ **Yarn:** Light worsted/DK
■ **Multiple:** Any number of sts
■ **Technique:** Crochet-on (page 122)

Special stitch

Waistcoat stitch (W-st): Insert hook between vertical V-shaped strands at front of indicated st and work sc.

Pattern

Rnd 1: Join color A in 2nd sc of any corner 3sc of base round, ch1, [3sc in corner st, W-st in each st to next corner st] 4 times, sl st in first sc made. End color A.

Rnd 2: Join color B in 2nd sc of corner 3sc, ch1, [3sc in corner st, W-st in each st to next corner st] 4 times, sl st in first sc made. End color B.

Rnd 3: Repeat row 2 using color C.

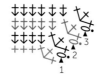

Base round

Whether you choose a sew-on or crochet-on edging pattern, always start by working a base round of single crochet around the afghan to provide a stable foundation (page 123). The base round is not included in the pattern instructions, but it is visible in the photographed crochet-on edgings and is shown in gray on the crochet-on edging charts.

Curvy

A
B
Base round

KEY

- ⬭ ch
- • sl st
- + sc
- ⋔ sc3tog
- ⊤ dc
- ◄ begin round

■ **Hook:** H-8 (5 mm)
■ **Yarn:** Light worsted/DK
■ **Multiple:** 4 + 3 + 4 corner sts
■ **Technique:** Crochet-on (page 122)

Special stitch

Single crochet 3 together (sc3tog): Work sc in each of next 3 sts but omit final yo of each sc, yo and pull through all 4 loops on hook.

Pattern

Rnd 1: Join color A in 2nd sc of any corner 3sc of base round, ch3 (counts as 1 dc), 6dc in same place, skip 1 st, sc in next st, *[skip 1 st, 5dc in next st, skip 1 st, sc in next st] to 1 st before next corner st, skip 1 st**, 7dc in corner st; rep from * twice more, then from * to ** once, sl st in top of beg ch3. End color A.

Rnd 2: Join color B in next st, ch1 and sc in same place, sc in next st, *3sc in next st, sc in next 2 sts, sc3tog in next 3 sts, [sc in next st, 3sc in next sc, sc in next st, sc3tog in next 3 sts] to 2nd dc of next corner**, sc in next 2 sts; rep from * twice more, then from * to ** once, sl st in first sc made. End color B.

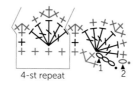

4-st repeat

Note

All of the photographs show the edgings as if they were hanging down from the bottom of an afghan. The charts are drawn to match the orientation of each edging as you are making it.

Spikes

A

KEY

◯ ch   ⊤ dc

• sl st

+ sc   ← direction of work

◀ begin row

- **Hook:** H-8 (5 mm)
- **Yarn:** Light worsted/DK
- **Technique:** Sew-on (page 123)

Pattern
Row 1: Ch7, 4dc in 7th ch from hook, ch3, turn, sl st in 2nd ch from hook and next ch, sc in next 4 sts, ch1, skip 1 ch, sc in next ch, turn.

Row 2: Ch4 (counts as 1 dc, ch1), 4dc in ch1sp, ch3, turn, sl st in 2nd ch from

hook and next ch, sc in next 4 sts, ch1, skip 1 ch, sc in next ch, turn.

Repeat row 2 until edging is the desired length.

Crab

A

Base round

KEY

◯ ch   ⨅ CS

• sl st   ◀ begin round

+ sc

- **Hook:** H-8 (5 mm)
- **Yarn:** Light worsted/DK
- **Multiple:** Any number of sts
- **Technique:** Crochet-on (page 122)

Special stitch
Crab stitch (CS)—reverse single crochet: Insert hook in next st to right of hook, yo and draw up a loop, yo and pull through both loops on hook.

Pattern
Rnd 1: Join color A in 2nd sc of any corner 3sc of base round, ch1 and CS in same place, CS in each st of base round, sl st in first CS made. End color A.

Arches

A

KEY

◯ ch   ⊤ dc

• sl st

+ sc   ← direction of work

◀ begin row

- **Hook:** H-8 (5 mm)
- **Yarn:** Light worsted/DK
- **Technique:** Sew-on (page 123)

Pattern
Row 1: Ch6, (2dc, ch2, 2dc) in 4th ch from hook, skip 1 ch, dc in last ch, turn.

Row 2: Ch3 (counts as 1 dc), skip 2 sts, (2dc, ch2, 2dc) in ch2sp, ch5, sl st in first dc of last row, turn, ch1, 10sc in ch5sp

just made, skip 2 sts, (2dc, ch2, 2dc) in ch2sp, skip 2 sts, dc in next st.

Repeat row 2 until edging is the desired length.

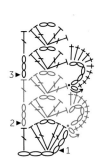

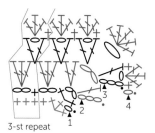

Skill level: |

Mosaic

A	E
B	F
C	G and base round
D	

KEY

○ ch

• sl st

+ sc

◄ begin round

- **Hook:** H-8 (5 mm)
- **Yarn:** Light worsted/DK
- **Multiple:** 2 + 1 + 4 corner sts
- **Technique:** Crochet-on (page 122)

Pattern

Rnd 1: Join color A in 2nd sc of any corner 3sc of base round, ch1 *(sc, ch2, sc) in corner st, ch1, skip 1 st, [sc in next st, ch1, skip 1 st] to next corner st; rep from * 3 times more, sl st in first sc made. End color A.

Rnd 2: Join color B in corner ch2sp, ch1, *(sc, ch2, sc) in ch2sp, ch1, skip 1 st, [sc in next ch1sp, ch1, skip 1 st] to next corner ch2sp; rep from * 3 more times, sl st in first sc made. End color B.

Rnd 3: Repeat round 2 using color C.

Rnd 4: Repeat round 2 using color D.

Rnd 5: Repeat round 2 using color E.

Rnd 6: Repeat round 2 using color F.

Rnd 7: Repeat round 2 using color G.

2-st repeat

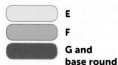

Skill level: |

Fancy

A	
B	
C	
D	
Base round	

KEY

○ ch

• sl st

+ sc

┬ dc

V V-st

◄ begin round

- **Hook:** H-8 (5 mm)
- **Yarn:** Light worsted/DK
- **Multiple:** 3 + 2 + 4 corner sts
- **Technique:** Crochet-on (page 122)

Special stitch

V-stitch (V-st): [Dc, ch1, dc] in place indicated.

Pattern

Rnd 1: Join color A in 2nd sc of any corner 3sc of base round, ch1, *(sc, ch2, sc) in corner st, ch2, skip 2 sts, [sc in next st, ch2, skip 2 sts] to next corner st; rep from * 3 times more, sl st in first sc made. End color A.

Rnd 2: Join color B in corner ch2sp, ch3 (counts as 1 dc), (dc, ch2, 2dc) in same place, *[skip 1 st, 3dc in ch2sp] to next corner ch2sp**, (2dc, ch2, 2dc) in corner ch2sp; rep from * twice more, then from * to ** once, sl st in top of beg ch3. End color B.

Rnd 3: Join color C in corner ch2sp, ch4 (counts as 1 dc, ch1), ([dc, ch1] twice, dc) in same place, *[V-st in gap between next 2 groups of dc] to next corner ch2sp**, (V-st, ch1, V-st) in corner ch2sp; rep from * twice more, then from * to ** once, sl st in 3rd ch of beg ch4. End color C.

Rnd 4: Join color D, ch1, sc in first st, *3dc in ch1sp, sc in next st, 5dc in corner ch1sp, sc in next st, 3dc in ch1sp, [sc between next 2 sts, 3dc in ch1sp] to last V-st before corner ch1sp**, sc between next 2 sts; rep from * twice more, then from* to ** once, sl st in first sc made. End color D.

3-st repeat

Skill level: 2

Flounce

A
B
C
Base round

KEY

○	ch	◄	begin round
•	sl st	←	turn work
+	sc		
V	V-st		
(bobble)	bobble		

- **Hook:** H-8 (5 mm)
- **Yarn:** Light worsted/DK
- **Multiple:** 2 + 1 + 4 corner sts
- **Technique:** Crochet-on (page 122)

Special stitches
V-stitch (V-st): [Dc, ch1, dc] in place indicated.

Bobble (BO): Work 5dc in place indicated but omit final yo of each dc, yo and pull through all 6 loops on hook.

Pattern
Rnd 1: Join color A in 2nd sc of any corner 3sc of base round, ch1, *(sc, ch2, sc) in corner st, ch1, skip 1 st, [sc in next st, ch1, skip 1 st] to next corner st; rep from * 3 times more, sl st in first sc made. End color A.

Rnd 2: Join color B in ch2sp, ch4 (counts as 1 dc, ch1), (dc, ch2, dc, ch1, dc) in same place, *[skip 1 st, V-st in ch1sp] to next corner ch2sp**, (V-st, ch2, V-st) in ch2sp; rep from * twice more, then from * to ** once, sl st in 3rd ch of beg ch4. End color B. Turn.

Rnd 3: Join color C, ch1, sc in first st, *BO in ch1sp, sc in next st, BO in corner ch2sp, sc in next st, BO in ch1sp, [sc between next 2 sts, BO in ch1sp] to last V-st before corner ch2sp**, sc between next 2 sts; rep from * twice more, then from * to ** once, sl st in first sc made. End color C.

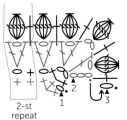

2-st repeat

Skill level: 2

Flowery

A

KEY

○	ch
•	sl st
(dc)	dc
(CL)	CL
◄	begin row
←	direction of work

- **Hook:** H-8 (5 mm)
- **Yarn:** Light worsted/DK
- **Technique:** Sew-on (page 123)

Special stitch
Cluster (CL): Work 3dc in place indicated but omit final yo of each dc, yo and pull through all 4 loops on hook.

Pattern
Row 1: Ch9, dc in 7th ch from hook (first ch4 counts as 1 dc, ch1), dc in next ch, 2dc in last ch, ch9, sl st in 5th ch from hook, turn, [ch2, CL, ch2, sl st] 3 times in ring, ch5, skip 1 dc, dc in next 3 sts, ch1, skip 1 ch, dc in next ch, turn.

Row 2: Ch4 (counts as 1 dc, ch1), skip 1 ch, dc in next 2 sts, 2dc in next st, ch9, sl st in 5th ch from hook, turn, [ch2, CL, ch2, sl st] 3 times in ring, ch5, skip 1 dc, dc in next 3 sts, ch1, skip 1 ch, dc in next ch, turn.

Repeat row 2 until edging is the desired length.

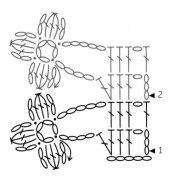

Ruffled

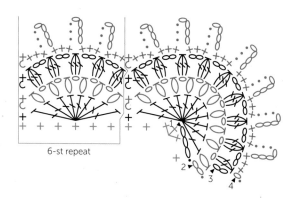

A
B
C
D
Base round

KEY

○ ch

• sl st

+ sc

ᵶ BPsc

Ŧ dc

ᵿ Puff

beg CL

CL

◄ begin round

- **Hook:** H-8 (5 mm)
- **Yarn:** Light worsted/DK
- **Multiple:** 6 + 5 + 4 corner sts
- **Technique:** Crochet-on (page 122)

Special stitches

Puff stitch (Puff): [Yo, insert hook in place indicated, yo and draw up a loop] twice, yo and pull through all 5 loops on hook.

Beginning cluster (beg CL): Ch2, work 2dc in place indicated but omit final yo of each dc, yo and pull through all 3 loops on hook.

Cluster (CL): Work 3dc in place indicated but omit final yo of each dc, yo and pull through all 4 loops on hook.

Pattern

Rnd 1: Join color A in 2nd sc of any corner 3sc of base round, ch3 (counts as 1 dc), 11dc in same place, skip 2 sts, sc in next st, *[skip 2 sts, 8dc in next st, skip 2 sts, sc in next st] to 2 sts before next corner st, skip 2 sts**, 12dc in corner st; rep from * twice more, then from * to ** once, sl st in top of beg ch3. End color A.

Rnd 2: Join color B, ch2 (does not count as a st), *skip 1 st, [Puff in next st, ch1] 9 times, Puff in next st, skip 1 st, BPsc in next st, [skip 1 st, (Puff in next st, ch1) 5 times, Puff in next st, skip 1 st, BPsc in next st] to next corner 12dc; rep from * 3 times more, sl st in top of first Puff made. End color B.

Rnd 3: Join color C in next ch1sp, beg CL in same place, ch2, [CL in next ch1sp, ch2] 7 times, CL in next ch1sp, skip next Puff, BPsc in next st, *skip next Puff, [CL in next ch1sp, ch2] 4 times, CL in next ch1sp, skip next Puff, BPsc in next st] to next corner 10 Puffs**, skip next Puff, [CL in next ch1sp, ch2] 8 times, CL in next ch1sp, skip next Puff, BPsc in next st; rep from * twice more, then from * to ** once, sl st in top of beg CL. End color C.

Rnd 4: Join color D in top of beg CL, ch1, *[3sc in ch2sp, ch4, sl st in 2nd ch from hook and next 2 ch] 7 times, 3sc in next ch2sp, skip next CL, BPsc in next st, [(3sc in ch2sp, ch4, sl st in 2nd ch from hook and next 2 ch) 3 times, 3sc in next ch2sp, skip next CL, BPsc in next st] to next corner 9CL; rep from * 3 times more, sl st in first sc made. End color D.

6-st repeat

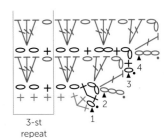

Skill level: 1

Granny

A
B
C
Base round

KEY

⬭ ch

• sl st

+ sc

T dc

◄ begin round

- **Hook:** H-8 (5 mm)
- **Yarn:** Light worsted/DK
- **Multiple:** 3 + 2 + 4 corner sts
- **Technique:** Crochet-on (page 122)

Pattern

Rnd 1: Join color A in 2nd sc of any corner 3sc of base round, ch1, *(sc, ch2, sc) in corner st, ch2, skip 2 sts, [sc in next st, ch2, skip 2 sts] to next corner st; rep from * 3 times more, sl st in first sc made. End color A.

Rnd 2: Join color B in corner ch2sp, ch3 (counts as 1 dc), (dc, ch2, 2dc) in same place, *[ch1, skip 1 st, 3dc in ch2sp] to next corner ch2sp, ch1, skip 1 st**, (2dc, ch2, 2dc) in corner ch2sp; rep from * twice more, then

from * to ** once, sl st in top of beg ch3. End color B.

Rnd 3: Join color A in corner ch2sp, ch1, *(sc, ch2, sc) in corner ch2sp, ch2, skip 2 sts, [sc in ch1sp, ch2, skip next dc group] to next corner ch2sp; rep from * 3 times more, sl st in first sc made. End color A.

Rnd 4: Repeat row 2 using color C.

3-st
repeat

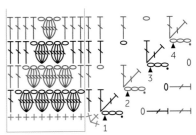

Skill level: 2

Prism

A
B
C
D
Base round

KEY

⬭ ch

• sl st

+ sc

T dc

🕸 PC

◄ begin round

- **Hook:** H-8 (5 mm)
- **Yarn:** Light worsted/DK
- **Multiple:** 10 + 1 + 4 corner sts
- **Technique:** Crochet-on (page 122)

Special stitch

Popcorn (PC): Work 5dc in place indicated, remove hook from loop, insert hook from front to back in top of first dc, pick up dropped loop and pull through loop on hook.

Pattern

Rnd 1: Join color A in 2nd sc of any corner 3sc of base round, ch3 (counts as 1 dc), 2dc in same place, *dc in next st, [ch1, skip 1 st, (PC in next st, ch1, skip 1 st) 4 times, dc in next st] to next corner st, 3dc in corner st; rep from * 3 times more, sl st in top of beg ch3. End color A.

Rnd 2: Join color B in next corner st, ch3 (counts as 1 dc), 2dc in same place,

*ch1, skip 1 st, dc in next st, [dc in ch1sp, ch1, (skip PC, PC in ch1sp, ch1) 3 times, skip PC, dc in ch1sp, dc in next st] to 1 st before next corner st, ch1, skip 1 st**, 3dc in corner st; rep from * twice more, then from * to ** once, sl st in top of beg ch3. End color B.

Rnd 3: Join color C in next corner st, ch3 (counts as 1 dc), 2dc in same place, *ch1, skip 1 st, dc in ch1sp, dc in next st, [dc in next st, dc in ch1sp, ch1, (skip PC, PC in ch1sp, ch1) twice, skip PC, dc in ch1sp, dc in next 2 sts] to last ch1sp before next corner st, dc in ch1sp, ch1, skip 1 st**, 3dc in corner st; rep from * twice more, then from * to ** once, sl st in top of beg ch3. End color C.

Rnd 4: Join color D in next corner st, ch3 (counts as 1 dc), 2dc in same place, *ch1, skip 1 st, dc in ch1sp, dc in next 2 sts, [dc in next 2 sts, dc in ch1sp, ch1, skip PC,

PC in ch1sp, ch1, skip PC, dc in ch1sp, dc in next 3 sts) to last (dc, ch1sp, dc) before next corner st, dc in next st, dc in ch1sp, ch1, skip 1 st**, 3dc in corner st; rep from * twice more, then from * to ** once, sl st in top of beg ch3. End color D.

10-st repeat

Techniques

Use this section to help brush up your skills or as an introductory guide if you are new to crochet. You will find plenty of practical advice and information on working the basic stitches and variations, guidance on how to read crochet patterns and follow charts, plus advice on joining blocks together and adding an edging to your afghan.

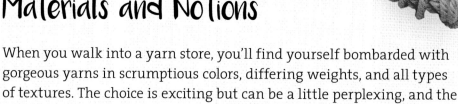

Materials and Notions

When you walk into a yarn store, you'll find yourself bombarded with gorgeous yarns in scrumptious colors, differing weights, and all types of textures. The choice is exciting but can be a little perplexing, and the same is true for hooks and accessories. Use this guide to find out what you need to get started.

Yarn choice

Suitable yarns for crochet range from very fine cotton to bulky wool. As a general rule, yarns that have a smooth texture and a medium or high twist are the easiest to work with. For making afghans, a medium-weight yarn is probably best, as it works up quickly, has good drape and stitch definition, and provides a warm and cozy blanket. All of the patterns in this book have been worked in DK/light worsted yarn.

Another thing to consider while standing in front of all that yarn is the fiber content and the kind of drape that you would like to achieve in your project. Before purchasing enough yarn to complete a project, it's a good idea to buy just one ball. Make a test swatch, wash it following the instructions on the ball band, block it to shape, and see whether you are comfortable using the yarn and whether it turns out how you'd intended.

Yarn fibers

Yarns come in a range of different fibers and fiber combinations.

Wool

Wool is an excellent choice for afghans. It is a resilient fiber that feels good to crochet with and has great stitch definition. If you are making a project that you would like to hand down to future generations and it is within your budget, wool is the fiber to use. Do find out whether or not the wool can be machine-washed.

Acrylic

Acrylic yarn is a perfect choice for beginners and popular with crochet enthusiasts. It's great for practicing stitches and techniques and testing color combinations. Acrylic yarns come in a huge array of colors and it is an affordable choice for your first project. Although acrylic can pill and lose its shape eventually, it does have the benefit of being machine-washable, making it a good choice for items that may require frequent washing.

Combination yarns

A yarn comprised of both wool and synthetic fiber is a dependable choice. Picking something that has a small percentage of synthetic fiber (for example, nylon or acrylic) makes a nice yarn to work with and launder, while still retaining the advantages of wool.

Cotton and cotton mixes

Cotton can present more of a challenge for beginners. It can be a little stiff to work with, but the stitches are crisp and neat. A cotton mix is usually softer to work with, yet still retains crisp, neat stitch definition. Afghans crocheted with cotton or a cotton mix are durable and cool, so are perfect for summer.

Novelty yarns

Although novelty yarns are tactile and enticing, they are not easy to work with. You can use a splash of novelty yarn to add some interest, but on the whole they are tricky to use and also hide the stitches.

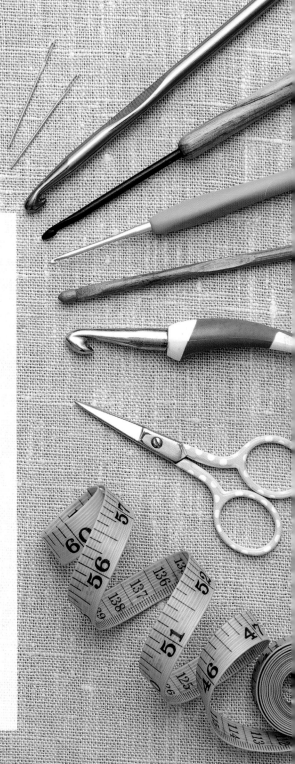

Crochet hooks

Hooks come in different sizes and materials. The material a hook is made from can affect your gauge. To start out, it's best to use aluminum hooks, as they have a pointed head and well-defined throat and work well with most yarns. Bamboo hooks are also pleasing to work with, but can be slippery with some yarns. Plastic hooks can be squeaky with synthetic yarns. You can also purchase hooks with soft-grip or wooden handles, which are great to work with, particularly if crochet becomes an obsession.

What size hook?

You may find that using the hook size recommended for a particular yarn or pattern isn't satisfactory, and your work may be too tight or too loose. Try different hook sizes until you are happy with the completed swatch. Ultimately, you want to use a hook and yarn weight that you are comfortable with—yarn/hook recommendations are not set in stone. Be aware that not all yarn labels give a recommended hook size. Use the recommended knitting needle size as a guide, or a hook one or two sizes bigger.

Notions

Although all you need to get started is a hook and some yarn, it's handy to have the following items in your work bag.

Scissors

Use a pair of small, sharp embroidery scissors.

Ruler and measuring tape

A rigid ruler is best for measuring gauge. A sturdy measuring tape is good for taking larger measurements.

Stitch markers

Split-ring markers are handy for keeping track of the first stitch of a row, particularly when starting out. Also use them to hold the working loop when you put your work down for the night.

Pins

Use rustproof, glass-headed pins for wet and steam blocking.

Needles

Yarn or tapestry needles are used for sewing seams and weaving in yarn ends. Choose needles with blunt ends to avoid splitting stitches. Yarn needles have different-sized eyes, so choose one that will accommodate the weight of yarn you will be using.

Starting and Finishing

Crochet can be worked in rows, beginning with a foundation chain, or in rounds, working outward from a foundation ring of chain stitches or a magic ring. See page 116 for a reminder of how to work the basic crochet stitches.

Holding the hook and yarn

The most common way of holding the hook is shown here, but if this doesn't feel comfortable to you, try grasping the flat section of the hook between your thumb and forefinger as if you were holding a knife.

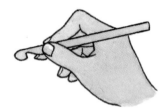

1 Holding the hook like a pen is the most widely used method. Center the tips of your right thumb and forefinger over the flat section of the hook.

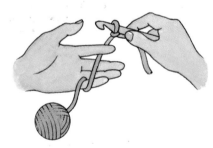

2 To control the supply and keep an even tension on the yarn, loop the short end of the yarn over your left forefinger, and take the yarn coming from the ball loosely around the little finger on the same hand. Use the middle finger on the same hand to help hold the work. If you are left-handed, hold the hook in your left hand and the yarn in your right.

Making a slip knot

1 Loop the yarn as shown, insert the hook into the loop, catch the yarn with the hook, and pull it through to make a loop over the hook.

2 Gently pull the yarn to tighten the loop around the hook and complete the slip knot.

Foundation chain

The pattern will tell you how many chains to make. This may be a specific number or a multiple. If a pattern tells you to make a multiple of 3 + 2, this does not mean make a multiple of 5. It means that you should make a multiple of 3 and then add 2 chains—e.g. 3 + 2, 6 + 2, 9 + 2, and so on. You may also be instructed to add a turning chain for the first row.

1 Holding the hook with the slip knot in your right hand and the yarn in your left hand, wrap the yarn over the hook. Draw the yarn through to make a new loop and complete the first chain stitch.

2 Repeat this process, drawing a new loop of yarn through the loop already on the hook until the foundation chain is the required length. Count each V-shaped loop on the front of the chain as one chain stitch, except for the loop on the hook, which is not counted. If your chain stitches are tight, try using a larger hook for the foundation chain. After every few stitches, move up the thumb and finger that are grasping the chain to keep the chain stitches even.

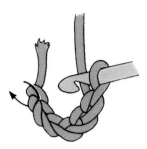

Foundation ring

1 Work a short length of foundation chain as specified in the pattern. Join the chains into a ring by working a slip stitch into the first chain of the foundation chain.

2 Work the first round of stitches into the center of the ring unless specified otherwise. At the end of the round, the final stitch is usually joined to the first stitch with a slip stitch.

Magic ring

Use this alternative to a foundation ring for working in the round when you want to avoid a hole in the center of your work. Wrap the yarn into a ring, insert the hook, and draw a loop through. Work the first round of crochet stitches into this ring, then pull the yarn tail tightly to close the ring.

Turning and starting chains

When working crochet, you will need to work a specific number of extra chains at the beginning of each row or round. When the work is turned at the end of a straight row, the extra chains are called a turning chain, and when they are worked at the beginning of a round, they are called a starting chain.

The extra chains bring the hook up to the correct height for the stitch you will be working next. The turning or starting chain is counted as the first stitch of the row or round, except when working single crochet where the single turning chain is ignored. A chain may be longer than the number required for the stitch, and in that case counts as one stitch plus a number of chains.

At the end of the row, the final stitch is usually worked into the turning chain at the beginning of the previous row. The final stitch may be worked into the top chain of the turning chain or into another specified stitch of the chain. At the end of a round, the final stitch is usually joined to the starting chain with a slip stitch.

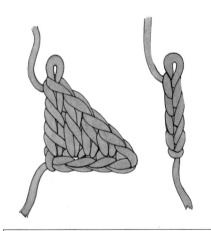

Number of turning chains

- **Single crochet (sc):** 1 turning chain
- **Half double crochet (hdc):** 2 turning chains
- **Double crochet (dc):** 3 turning chains
- **Treble crochet (tr):** 4 turning chains
- **Double treble crochet (dtr):** 5 turning chains
- **Triple treble crochet (trtr):** 6 turning chains

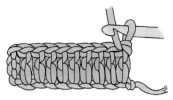

Fastening off

When you have completed your crochet, cut the yarn about 6 in. (15 cm) from the last stitch. Wrap the yarn over the hook and draw the yarn end through the loop on the hook. Gently pull the yarn to tighten the last stitch, then weave in the yarn end.

Finishing the last round

For a neater finish, don't use a slip stitch to join the last stitch of the final round to the first stitch of the round. Instead, fasten off the yarn after the last stitch, thread a yarn needle with the end of yarn, and pass it under the top loops of the first stitch of the round and back through the center of the last stitch.

Weaving in ends

At the end of making your project, you will need to weave in any yarn ends from changing colors and sewing seams. For crochet worked in rows, use a yarn needle to sew in ends diagonally on the wrong side. For crochet worked in rounds, sew in ends under stitches for a couple of inches. If the pattern doesn't allow this, sew under a few stitches, then up through the back of a stitch, and under a few more stitches on the next row.

Basic Stitches

All crochet stitches are based on a loop pulled through another loop by a hook. There are only a few stitches to master, each of a different length. Here is a concise guide to the basic stitches used to make the afghans.

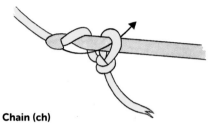

Chain (ch)
Wrap the yarn over the hook and pull it through the loop on the hook to form a new loop on the hook.

Extended single crochet (Ext sc)
Insert the hook into the specified stitch, yarn over hook, and pull it through the stitch (2 loops on hook). Chain 1. Yarn over hook and pull it through both loops.

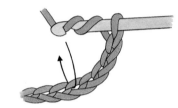

Treble crochet (tr)
Yarn over hook twice, insert the hook into the specified stitch, yarn over hook, and pull it through the stitch (4 loops on hook). *Yarn over hook and pull it through two loops; repeat from * twice more.

Slip stitch (sl st)
Insert the hook into the specified stitch, wrap the yarn over the hook, and pull it through the stitch and the loop on the hook.

Half double crochet (hdc)
Yarn over hook, insert the hook into the specified stitch, yarn over hook, and pull it through the stitch (3 loops on hook). Yarn over hook and pull it through all three loops.

Single crochet (sc)
Insert the hook into the specified stitch, wrap the yarn over the hook, and pull it through the stitch (2 loops on hook). Yarn over hook and pull it through both loops.

Double crochet (dc)
Yarn over hook, insert the hook into the specified stitch, yarn over hook, and pull it through the stitch (3 loops on hook). *Yarn over hook and pull it through two loops; repeat from * once more.

Making taller stitches

You can make taller stitches by wrapping the yarn over the hook as many times as you wish before inserting the hook into the specified stitch. For example, wrap the yarn over the hook three times to make a double treble crochet (dtr). Make four wraps for a triple treble crochet (trtr) and so on. Complete the stitch in the same way as treble crochet, working off two loops at a time in the usual way.

Simple Stitch Variations

Basic stitches may be varied in many ways to achieve different effects. These simple variations are all made by inserting the hook in different places in the crochet to work the stitches.

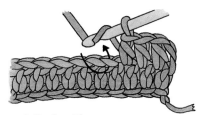

Through the front loop
Rather than inserting the hook under both top loops to work the next stitch in the usual way, insert it only under the front loop.

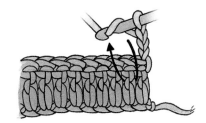

Around the front post (FP)
Work around the stem of the stitch, inserting the hook from front to back, around the post, and to the front again.

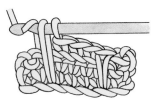

Into a row below (spike stitch)
Spike stitches are made by inserting the hook one or more rows below the previous row. To work a single crochet spike stitch, for example, insert the hook as directed by the pattern, wrap the yarn over the hook and draw it through, lengthen the loop to the height of the working row, then complete the stitch.

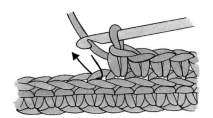

Through the back loop
Rather than inserting the hook under both top loops to work the next stitch in the usual way, insert it only under the back loop.

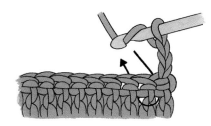

Around the back post (BP)
Work around the stem of the stitch, inserting the hook from back to front, around the post, and to the back again.

Into the "V" (waistcoat stitch—W-st)
This variation is worked into the right side of a single crochet stitch. Instead of inserting the hook under the top two loops of the stitch, this time insert it into the "V" formed by the two vertical strands at the front of the stitch.

There should be three strands of yarn above the hook when you do this, two from the top of the stitch and one from the back of the stitch. Complete the single crochet in the usual way.

Into a chain space (chsp)
Insert the hook into the space below a chain or chains. Here, a tr is being worked into a ch1sp.

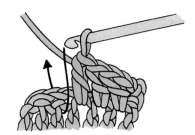

Into a stitch space
Insert the hook between the stitches of the previous row, instead of into a stitch itself.

Special Stitches

By working multiple stitches in the same place or working several stitches together at the top, or a combination of both, you can create interesting shapes, patterns, and textures. The turning or starting chain may be counted as the first stitch of a cluster, bobble, popcorn, or puff stitch.

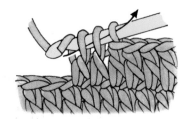

Decrease (e.g. sc2tog, dc3tog)

One or two stitches can be decreased by working two or three incomplete stitches together. Work the specified number of stitches, omitting the final stage (the last yarn over) of each stitch so that the last loop of each stitch remains on the hook. Wrap the yarn over the hook and draw it through all of the loops on the hook. The method is the same for all the basic crochet stitches.

Cluster (CL)

A cluster can be made from a multiple of any of the basic crochet stitches. Work the specified number of stitches in the places indicated in the pattern, omitting the final stage of each stitch so that the last loop of each stitch remains on the hook. Wrap the yarn over the hook and draw it through all of the loops on the hook.

Popcorn (PC)

A popcorn is a group of double crochet or longer stitches worked in the same place, and then folded and closed at the top so that the popcorn is raised from the background stitches. Work the specified number of stitches in the same place. Take the hook out of the working loop and insert it under both top loops of the first stitch of the popcorn. Pick up the working loop with the hook and draw it through to fold the group of stitches and close the popcorn at the top.

Increase (e.g. 5dc in next ch)

This technique is used to increase the total number of stitches when shaping an item, or to create a decorative effect such as a shell. Simply work the required number of stitches in the same place. Increases may be worked at the edges of flat pieces, or at any point along a row or round.

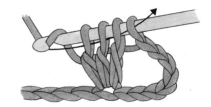

Bobble (BO)

A bobble is a group of between three and six double crochet or longer stitches worked in the same place and closed at the top. Work the specified number of stitches, omitting the final stage of each stitch so that the last loop of each stitch remains on the hook. Wrap the yarn over the hook and draw it through all of the loops on the hook.

Puff stitch

A puff stitch is a cluster of half double crochet stitches worked in the same place. Work the specified number of stitches, omitting the final stage of each stitch so that two loops of each one remain on the hook. Wrap the yarn over hook and draw it through all of the loops on the hook.

Colorwork

Most of the afghan patterns use a single color for each row or round, with the new color being joined at the end of a row or round. Tapestry and intarsia designs involve using multiple colors across the row. In tapestry crochet, the unworked color is carried behind the row and woven in. Intarsia crochet features large and sometimes irregularly shaped sections of different colors, and each section is worked with a separate ball of yarn.

Changing color on a row
When working the last stitch of the old color, omit the final stage (the last yarn over) to leave the stitch incomplete. Wrap the new yarn over the hook and draw it through all of the loops on the hook to complete the stitch. The new yarn will form the top loops of the next stitch in the new color.

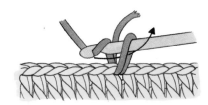

Changing color on a round
Method 1: When joining the last stitch of the round to the first stitch using a slip stitch, work the joining slip stitch using the new color. Method 2 (above): Insert the hook where required and draw up a loop of the new color, leaving a 4 in. (10 cm) tail. Work the specified number of starting chains. Continue with the new yarn.

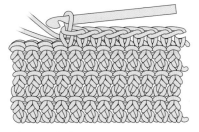

Tapestry crochet
1 Change to the new color (pink) in the usual way. Continue following the pattern, carrying the unused yarn (blue) along the top of the previous row at the back of the work and crocheting over it. After the next color change, continue to carry and work over the unused yarn in the same way.

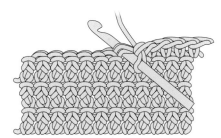

2 On the next and all other rows, insert the hook under the carried yarn and into the stitch to lock the carried yarn in place.

Intarsia crochet
Use a separate ball or bobbin of yarn for each area of color. If the same color is used twice across the row, you will need two separate balls of it.

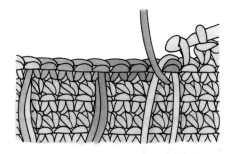

1 Follow the pattern, changing colors where indicated in the usual way and dropping the unused yarns to the wrong side of the work. At each color change on subsequent rows, make sure that you loop the new yarn around the old one on the wrong side of the work to prevent holes.

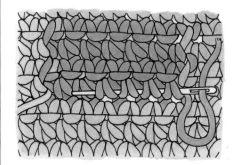

2 Take extra care when dealing with all the yarn ends on a piece of intarsia. Carefully weave each end into an area of crochet worked in the same color so that it will not be visible on the right side.

Reading Patterns and Charts

With all those symbols, abbreviations, and charts, crochet can seem daunting and complex to begin with. A little explanation, though, and all becomes clear.

Abbreviations are used to make crochet patterns quicker and easier to follow. Abbreviations and chart symbols may vary from one pattern publisher to another, so always check that you understand the system in use before commencing work. Some patterns use special abbreviations and symbols and specific stitch instructions, and these are explained with each pattern.

Understanding symbols

Symbol	Meaning
*	Start of repeat
**	End of last repeat
[ ]	Repeat the instructions within the brackets the stated number of times
( )	Can either be explanatory (counts as 1 dc) or can be read as a group of stitches worked in the same place (dc, ch2, dc)
▶	An arrowhead indicates the beginning of a row or round

Symbols joined at top

 A group of symbols joined at the top should be worked together at the top, as in cluster stitches and for decreasing (e.g. sc2tog, dc3tog)

Symbols joined at base

 Symbols joined at the base should all be worked into the same stitch below

Symbols joined at top and base

 Sometimes a group of stitches are joined at both top and bottom, making a puff, bobble, or popcorn

Symbols on a curve

 Sometimes symbols are drawn at an angle, depending on the construction of the stitch pattern

Distorted symbols

 Some symbols may be lengthened, curved, or spiked, to indicate where the hook is inserted below

Symbols and abbreviations

Symbol	Meaning	Abbreviation
◯	Chain	ch
•	Slip stitch	sl st
+	Single crochet	sc
T	Half double crochet	hdc
↑	Double crochet	dc
↑	Treble crochet	tr
↑	Double treble crochet	dtr
↑	Triple treble crochet	trtr
⋀ e.g. cluster of 3dc	Cluster	CL
e.g. bobble of 5dc	Bobble	BO
e.g. puff of 5hdc	Puff stitch	Puff
e.g. popcorn of 5dc	Popcorn	PC
⊼ e.g. sc through back loop	Through back loop	–
⊔ e.g. hdc through front loop	Through front loop	–
⌡	Back post	BP
⌡	Front post	FP
–	Beginning	beg
–	Chain space	chsp
–	Repeat	rep
–	Right side / Wrong side	RS / WS
–	Stitch(es)	st(s)
–	Together	tog
–	Yarn over	yo

Reading charts

Each design in this book is accompanied by a chart, which should be read together with the written instructions. Once you are used to the symbols, they are quick and easy to follow. All charts are read from the right side.

Charts in rows

- Right-side rows start at the right, and are read from right to left.
- Wrong-side rows start at the left, and are read from left to right.
- The beginning of each row is indicated by an arrow.

Charts in rounds

These charts begin at the center, and each round is read counterclockwise, in the same direction as working. The beginning of each round is indicated by an arrow. Some charts have been stretched to show all the stitches.

Calculating yarn amounts

Each of the block patterns in this book provides the amount of yarn required to make one block. Multiply this amount by the number of blocks you plan to make and round up to the nearest yard or meter. On page 124, you will find yarn quantities for three sizes of afghan for all 40 patterns. These quantities are approximate and based on using DK/light worsted yarn and the size of hook recommended for the pattern.

The best way to calculate how much yarn you will need is to make a few blocks or work a few repeats of a pattern in the yarn and color combination you intend to use, then unravel them. Measure the amount of yarn used for each color, take the average length, and multiply by the number of blocks or pattern repeats you intend to make. Add extra yarn for joining blocks and working edgings.

Gauge and Blocking

It's important to crochet a test swatch before you start your project to establish gauge. To finish off your afghan neatly, you will need to block it. You can use the gauge swatch to test blocking and cleaning methods.

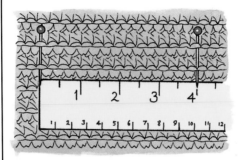

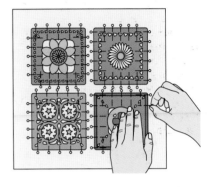

Measuring gauge

No two people will crochet to the exact same gauge, even when working with identical yarn and hooks. Always make a test swatch before starting a project so that you can compare your gauge with the pattern gauge and get an idea of how the finished project will feel and drape. It's also useful for testing out different color combinations.

To test your gauge, make a sample swatch in the yarn you intend to use following the pattern directions. Block the sample and then measure again. If your swatch is larger, try making another using a smaller hook. If your swatch is smaller, try making another using a bigger hook. Also do this if the fabric feels too loose and floppy or too dense and rigid. Keep trying until you find a hook size that will give you the required gauge, or until you are happy with the drape and feel of your work. Ultimately, it's more important that you use a hook and yarn you are comfortable with than that you rigidly follow the pattern instructions.

Blocking

Blocking is crucial to set the stitches and even out the piece. Choose a method based on the care label of the yarn. When in doubt, use the wet method. Use an ironing board or old quilt, or make a blocking board by securing one or two layers of quilter's batting, covered with a sheet of cotton fabric, over a flat board.

Wet method—acrylic and wool/acrylic mix

Using rustproof pins, pin the crochet fabric to the correct measurements on a flat surface and dampen using a spray bottle of cold water. Pat the fabric to help the moisture penetrate. Ease stitches into position, keeping rows and stitches straight. Allow to dry before removing the pins.

Steam method—wools and cottons

Pin out the fabric as above. For fabric with raised stitches, pin it right side up to avoid squashing the stitches; otherwise, pin it wrong side up. Steam lightly, holding the iron 1 in. (2.5 cm) above the fabric. Allow the steam to penetrate for several seconds. It is safer to avoid pressing, but if you choose to do so, cover with a clean towel or cloth first.

Joining and Edging

If you are making your afghan from a block pattern, you will need to sew or crochet the blocks together before adding an edging. A crochet edging does not just finish off a project with style, but it also helps the afghan to hold its shape and keeps the edges from stretching. See page 100 for a selection of edging patterns.

Joining blocks

Blocks can be joined by sewing or by crochet. Pin seams together to help match up the blocks and give a neat finish. Use the same yarn that you used for the blocks, or a finer yarn, preferably with the same fiber content.

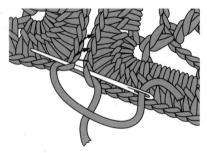

Overcasting
Using a yarn needle, sew through the back or front loops of corresponding stitches. For extra strength, work two stitches into the end loops.

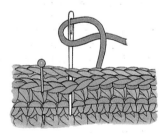

Backstitch
Hold the blocks with right sides together. Using a yarn needle, work a line of backstitches along the edge.

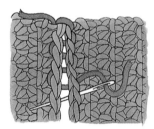

Mattress stitch
Lay the blocks wrong side up and with edges touching. Using a yarn needle, weave back and forth around the centers of the stitches, without pulling the stitches too tight.

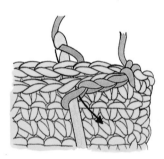

Crochet seams
Join the blocks with wrong sides together for a visible seam, or with right sides together for an invisible one. Work a row of slip stitch (above) or single crochet through both top loops of each block. When using this method along the side edges of blocks worked in rows, work enough evenly spaced stitches so that the seam is not too tight.

Crochet-on edgings

Calculate how many stitches the edging pattern needs, including corners. When working the base round (page 123), increase or decrease the number of stitches along each edge of the afghan to match the edging pattern you have chosen. Make sure increase or decrease stitches are evenly spaced to avoid puckering. Using markers to indicate where pattern repeats will lie will help you to visualize it.

Crochet-on edging calculations
Each edging pattern starts in the corner stitch of the base round and includes instructions for working the corners. Some designs require a specific multiple of stitches in order to work the pattern repeat. This is written in the pattern instructions as:

- Multiple: x + x + 4 corner sts

The corner stitches will be the second single crochet of each corner of the base round, so after working your base round you will have four corner stitches (1 st at each corner). If the pattern requires a multiple of 3 + 2 + 4 corner stitches, you should have a multiple of 3 stitches with 2 stitches remaining along each edge (e.g. 3 + 2, 6 + 2, 9 + 2, and so on), plus 4 corner stitches. Count the stitches along each edge between the corner stitches to check you have the correct number. If you do not, you can work another base round, decreasing or adding stitches evenly as needed.

Sew-on edgings

Sew-on edgings are usually worked sideways by working a few stitches on each row for the length required. Make the edging longer than it appears to need to be. If possible, sew the edging in place as you make it, adding any extra length as you go.

Calculating how much you need

When calculating the amount you need, add about an extra 2–4 in. (5–10 cm) of edging for every 40 in. (100 cm) of afghan edge, allowing extra length to turn corners. Try out the edging on your gauge swatch to help you calculate the correct number of stitches you will need for the edging to sit correctly around corners.

Attaching sew-on edgings

Don't fasten off the yarn in case you need to make adjustments to the length of the edging. Hold the working loop of the edging with a marker to keep it from unraveling. Place the edge of the afghan and the edge of the edging so that the right sides of both are facing you, with the edging on top. Pin in place and sew on the edging using overcast stitch through the front loops. Make any adjustments to the length of the edging, then fasten off the yarn and use the tail to join the two ends of the border together.

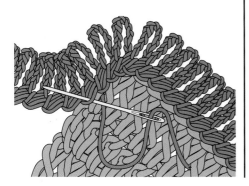

Base round

This is the most important step in working your edgings. A base round provides the edging with a good, stable foundation. It helps to even out untidy edges at row ends and any uneven stitches. Make the base round by crocheting one round of single crochet around the afghan, working three stitches in each corner. Work a base round for both crochet-on and sew-on edgings.

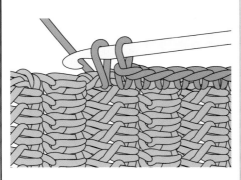

Along sides of row ends

When working on the side edge of an afghan worked in rows, insert the hook under two threads of the first (or last) stitch of each row. Place the stitches an even distance apart along the edge. Try a short length to test the number of stitches required for a flat result. As a guide:
- **Rows of sc:** 1sc in side edge of each row.
- **Rows of hdc:** 3sc in side edge of every two rows.
- **Rows of dc:** 2sc in side edge of each row.
- **Rows of tr:** 3sc in side edge of each row.

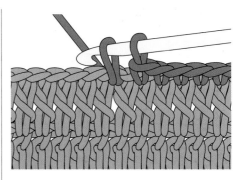

Across the top or bottom edge

When working across the top of a row, work 1sc into each stitch as you would if working another row. When working across the bottom edge of chain stitches, work 1sc in the remaining loop of each foundation chain.

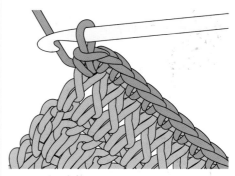

Around corners

You will need to add a couple of stitches at each corner to allow the base round to turn the corner without distorting the afghan. As a guide, corners are normally turned by working 3sc (or sc, hdc, sc) into the corner. If you find the base round is too wavy or too taut after it has been completed, it will probably get worse once the rest of the edging has been worked. Take time at this point to pull out the base round and redo it using fewer stitches if the edge is too wavy, or using more stitches if the edge is too taut.

Yarn Quantities and Colors

Approximate yarn quantities are listed here for making three different sizes of afghan, excluding edgings. All block patterns should match these afghan sizes if you match the stated gauge. For row-by-row patterns, the table also provides the length of foundation chain and number of whole repeats to work in order to match these afghan sizes as closely as possible. Adjust as necessary to suit your personal gauge.

- **Baby blanket:** 36 x 36 in. (90 x 90 cm); if using a square block pattern, make 36 blocks and join in 6 rows of 6 blocks.
- **Throw:** 60 x 72 in. (150 x 180 cm); if using a square block pattern, make 120 blocks and join in 12 rows of 10 blocks.
- **Bedspread:** 84 x 90 in. (210 x 225 cm); if using a square block pattern, make 210 blocks and join in 15 rows of 14 blocks.

- **Cascade colors:** All yarns are from Cascade Yarns' DK-weight 220 Superwash range. Please use the color numbers provided as a guide only and be sure to check exact colors with your yarn supplier before purchasing.
- **Quantities:** Follow the advice on page 121 to calculate yarn amounts for other sizes or afghan and to double-check the quantities below using your chosen yarn and hook.

Pattern	Baby blanket	Throw	Bedspread	Cascade colors
Bobble Along p.10	Ch129; repeats = 62 wide x 5 high; A 49 yd (44 m), B 34 yd (31 m), C 156 yd (142 m), D 34 yd (31 m), E 95 yd (86 m), F 188 yd (171 m), G 128 yd (117 m), H 188 yd (171 m)	Ch213; repeats = 104 wide x 10 high; A 145 yd (132 m), B 103 yd (94 m), C 466 yd (426 m), D 103 yd (94 m), E 283 yd (258 m), F 564 yd (515 m), G 384 yd (351 m), H 564 yd (515 m)	Ch297; repeats = 146 wide x 12 high; A 243 yd (222 m), B 174 yd (159 m), C 789 yd (721 m), D 174 yd (159 m), E 477 yd (436 m), F 954 yd (872 m), G 650 yd (594 m), H 954 yd (872 m)	A 844, B 851, C 1942, D 871, E 837, F 839, G 824, H 827
Band of Hearts p.12	Ch83; repeats = 20 wide x 5 high; A 188 yd (171 m), B 50 yd (45 m), C 113 yd (103 m), D 280 yd (256 m), E 64 yd (58 m), F 95 yd (86 m), G 95 yd (86 m), H 101 yd (92 m)	Ch139; repeats = 34 wide x 10 high; A 632 yd (577 m), B 163 yd (149 m), C 379 yd (346 m), D 939 yd (858 m), E 217 yd (198 m), F 317 yd (289 m), G 317 yd (289 m), H 338 yd (309 m)	Ch191; repeats = 47 wide x 12 high; A 1045 yd (955 m), B 267 yd (244 m), C 625 yd (571 m), D 1549 yd (1416 m), E 359 yd (328 m), F 523 yd (478 m), G 523 yd (478 m), H 559 yd (511 m)	A 816, B 886, C 817, D 875, E 838, F 903, G 1942, H 879
Baby Diamonds p.14	Ch122; repeats = 10 wide x 8 high; A 325 yd (297 m), B 315 yd (288 m), C 321 yd (293 m), D 315 yd (288 m)	Ch206; repeats = 17 wide x 16 high; A 1089 yd (995 m), B 1072 yd (980 m), C 1082 yd (989 m), D 1072 yd (980 m)	Ch290; repeats = 24 wide x 21 high; A 2008 yd (1836 m), B 1985 yd (1815 m), C 1999 yd (1827 m), D 1985 yd (1815 m)	A 847, B 836, C 851, D 826
Dazzling Daisy p.16	A 60 yd (54 m), B 99 yd (90 m), C 256 yd (234 m), D 512 yd (468 m), E 315 yd (288 m)	A 197 yd (180 m), B 329 yd (300 m), C 854 yd (780 m), D 1707 yd (1560 m), E 1050 yd (960 m)	A 345 yd (315 m), B 575 yd (525 m), C 1493 yd (1365 m), D 2986 yd (2730 m), E 1838 yd (1680 m)	A 914a, B 825, C 851, D 1971, E 1967
Granny's Corner p.18	A 60 yd (54 m), B 375 yd (342 m), C 79 yd (72 m), D 315 yd (288 m), E 119 yd (108 m), F 138 yd (126 m), G 158 yd (144 m)	A 197 yd (180 m), B 1247 yd (1140 m), C 263 yd (240 m), D 1050 yd (960 m), E 394 yd (360 m), F 460 yd (420 m), G 525 yd (480 m)	A 345 yd (315 m), B 2182 yd (1995 m), C 460 yd (420 m), D 1838 yd (1680 m), E 689 yd (630 m), F 804 yd (735 m), G 919 yd (840 m)	A 825, B 808, C 820, D 887, E 849, F 896, G 1986
Interrupted p.20	A 512 yd (468 m), B 119 yd (108 m), C 79 yd (72 m), D 276 yd (252 m), E 276 yd (252 m)	A 1707 yd (1560 m), B 394 yd (360 m), C 263 yd (240 m), D 919 yd (840 m), E 919 yd (840 m)	A 2986 yd (2730 m), B 689 yd (630 m), C 460 yd (420 m), D 1608 yd (1470 m), E 1608 yd (1470 m)	A 1973, B 816, C 1952, D 887, E 903
Log Cabin p.22	A 79 yd (72 m), B 99 yd (90 m), C 138 yd (126 m), D 178 yd (162 m), E 217 yd (198 m), F 355 yd (324 m), G 434 yd (396 m)	A 263 yd (240 m), B 329 yd (300 m), C 460 yd (420 m), D 591 yd (540 m), E 722 yd (660 m), F 1182 yd (1080 m), G 1444 yd (1320 m)	A 460 yd (420 m), B 575 yd (525 m), C 804 yd (735 m), D 1034 yd (945 m), E 1264 yd (1155 m), F 2067 yd (1890 m), G 2527 yd (2310 m)	A 1921, B 820, C 851, D 827, E 849, F 903, G 848

Pattern	Baby blanket	Throw	Bedspread	Cascade colors
Holi Festival Blanket p.24	Ch113; repeats = 36 wide x 5 high; A–L 75 yd (68 m) each	Ch185; repeats = 60 wide x 10 high; A–L 247 yd (225 m) each	Ch257; repeats = 84 wide x 12 high; A–L 414 yd (378 m) each	A 885, B 844, C 887, D 820, E 825, F 807, G 1921, H 871, I 851, J 1952, K 847, L 875
Neon Frills p.28	Ch184; repeats = 90 wide x 30 high; A 1065 yd (973 m), B–D 178 yd (162 m) each	Ch306; repeats = 151 wide x 60 high; A 1628 yd (3317 m), B–D 595 yd (544 m) each	Ch428; repeats = 212 wide x 74 high; A 6345 yd (5801 m), B–D 1002 yd (916 m) each	A 816, B 1973, C 1952, D 851
Pastel Rows p.30	A–D 197 yd (180 m) each, E 355 yd (324 m)	A–D 657 yd (600 m) each, E 1182 yd (1080 m)	A–D 1149 yd (1050 m) each, E 1182 yd (1080 m)	A 1967, B 850, C 875, D 897, E 901
Reversi p.32	A 79 yd (72 m), B 158 yd (144 m), C 237 yd (216 m), D 315 yd (288 m), E 394 yd (360 m), F 473 yd (432 m)	A 263 yd (240 m), B 525 yd (480 m), C 788 yd (720 m), D 1050 yd (960 m), E 1313 yd (1200 m), F 1575 yd (1440 m)	A 460 yd (420 m), B 919 yd (840 m), C 1378 yd (1260 m), D 1838 yd (1680 m), E 2297 yd (2100 m), F 2756 yd (2520 m)	A 817, B 1915, C 1941, D 1940, E 903, F 807
Rice Field p.34	Ch122; repeats = 60 wide x 30 high; A–D 397 yd (363 m) each	Ch204; repeats = 101 wide x 61 high; A–D 1355 yd (1239 m) each	Ch286; repeats = 142 wide x 76 high; A–D 2369 yd (2166 m) each	A 887, B 1971, C 228, D 807
Textured Ripple p.36	Ch124; repeats = 30 wide x 8 high; A–G 283 yd (258 m) each	Ch208; repeats = 51 wide x 16 high; A–G 961 yd (878 m) each	Ch288; repeats = 71 wide x 20 high; A–G 1670 yd (1527 m) each	A 825, B 834, C 914a, D 1967, E 844, F 1973, G 850
Carnival p.38	Ch116; repeats = 11 wide x 11 high; A, C, E, G 194 yd (177 m) each, B, D, F 195 yd (178 m) each	Ch196; repeats = 19 wide x 22 high; A, C, E, G 687 yd (628 m) each, B, D, F 688 yd (629 m) each	Ch266; repeats = 26 wide x 28 high; A, C, E, G 1222 yd (1117 m) each, B, D, F 1223 yd (1118 m) each	A 810, B 851, C 825, D 903, E 807, F 1967, G 1971
Checkmate p.40	Ch121; repeats = 6 wide x 6 high; A–B 473 yd (432 m) each	Ch201; repeats = 10 wide x 12 high; A–B 1575 yd (1440 m) each	Ch281; repeats = 14 wide x 15 high; A–B 2756 yd (2520 m) each	A 848, B 820
Diagonals Baby Blanket p.42	A 138 yd (126 m), B 670 yd (612 m), C 630 yd (576 m), D 138 yd (126 m)	A 460 yd (420 m), B 2231 yd (2040 m), C 2100 yd (1920 m), D 460 yd (420 m)	A 804 yd (735 m), B 3905 yd (3570 m), C 3675 yd (3360 m), D 804 yd (735 m)	A 1952, B 871, C 849, D 877
Coral Shells p.46	Ch114; repeats = 18 wide x 6 high; A 188 yd (171 m), B 155 yd (141 m), C 274 yd (250 m), D 212 yd (193 m), E 215 yd (196 m)	Ch186; repeats = 30 wide x 12 high; A 619 yd (566 m), B 506 yd (462 m), C 894 yd (817 m), D 692 yd (632 m), E 699 yd (639 m)	Ch258; repeats = 42 wide x 15 high; A 1082 yd (989 m), B 881 yd (805 m), C 1552 yd (1419 m), D 1203 yd (1100 m), E 2274 yd (2079 m)	A 874, B 901, C 1973, D 827, E 1942
Strawberries and Cream p.48	A 571 yd (522 m), B 729 yd (666 m)	A 1903 yd (1740 m), B 2428 yd (2220 m)	A 3331 yd (3045 m), B 4249 yd (3885 m)	A 910a, B 1922
Fizzy Mint p.50	A 197 yd (180 m), B 276 yd (252 m), C 375 yd (342 m), D 276 yd (252 m)	A 657 yd (600 m), B 919 yd (840 m), C 1247 yd (1140 m), D 919 yd (840 m)	A 1149 yd (1050 m), B 1608 yd (1470 m), C 2182 yd (1995 m), D 1608 yd (1470 m)	A 834, B 817, C 227, D 850

Pattern	Baby blanket	Throw	Bedspread	Cascade colors
Granny Stripes p.52	Ch113; repeats = 36 wide x 5 high; A 286 yd (261 m), B–D 268 yd (245 m) each, E 67 yd (61 m)	Ch185; repeats = 60 wide x 9 high; A 847 yd (774 ·m), B–D 791 yd (723 m) each, E 198 yd (181 m)	Ch260; repeats = 85 wide x 12 high; A 1477 yd (1350 m), B–D 1383 yd (1264 m) each, E 345 yd (315 m)	A 814, B 227, C 887, D 821, E 808
Lily Pad p.54	A 60 yd (54 m), B 158 yd (144 m), C 138 yd (126 m), D 217 yd (198 m), E 256 yd (234 m), F 178 yd (162 m)	A 197 yd (180 m), B 525 yd (480 m), C 460 yd (420 m), D 722 yd (660 m), E 854 yd (780 m), F 591 yd (540 m)	A 345 yd (315 m), B 919 yd (840 m), C 804 yd (735 m), D 1264 yd (1155 m), E 1493 yd (135 m), F 1034 yd (945 m)	A 901, B 1921, C 817, D 887, E 802, F 1985
Luxor p.56	A 355 yd (324 m), B 99 yd (90 m), C 178 yd (162 m), D 237 yd (216 m), E 296 yd (270 m)	A 1182 yd (1080 m), B 329 yd (300 m), C 591 yd (540 m), D 788 yd (720 m), E 985 yd (900 m)	A 2067 yd (1890 m), B 575 yd (525 m), C 1034 yd (945 m), D 1378 yd (1260 m), E 1723 yd (1575 m)	A 825, B 802, C 887, D 844, E 1971
Phoenix p.58	A 60 yd (54 m), B 99 yd (90 m), C 158 yd (144 m), D 237 yd (216 m), E 493 yd (450 m)	A 197 yd (180 m), B 329 yd (300 m), C 525 yd (480 m), D 788 yd (720 m), E 1641 yd (1500 m)	A 345 yd (315 m), B 575 yd (525 m), C 919 yd (840 m), D 1378 yd (1260 m), E 2871 yd (2625 m)	A 808, B 821, C 1952, D 892, E 816
Granny Quilt p.60	18 blocks (3 rows of 6 blocks); A 99 yd (90 m), B 178 yd (162 m), C 217 yd (198 m), D 237 yd (216 m), E 266 yd (243 m), F 286 yd (261 m)	60 blocks (5 rows of 12 blocks); A 329 yd (300 m), B 591 yd (540 m), C 722 yd (660 m), D 788 yd (720 m), E 886 yd (810 m), F 952 yd (870 m)	105 blocks (7 rows of 15 blocks); A 575 yd (525 m), B 1034 yd (945 m), C 1264 yd (1155 m), D 1378 yd (1260 m), E 1551 yd (1418 m), F 1666 yd (1523 m)	A 820, B 834, C 914a, D 851, E 842, F 1986
Purplicious p.64	Ch134; repeats = 26 wide x 5 high; A 758 yd (693 m), B–F 669 yd (611 m) each	Ch224; repeats = 44 wide x 10 high; A 2500 yd (2286 m), B–F 220 yd (201 m) each	Ch309; repeats = 61 wide x 12 high; A 4182 yd (3824 m), B–F 367 yd (335 m) each	A 1986, B 850, C 901, D 849, E 820, F 1952
Bobble Band p.66	Ch149; repeats = 36 wide x 9 high; A 652 yd (596 m), B 146 yd (133 m), C 399 yd (364 m), D 146 yd (133 m)	Ch245; repeats = 60 wide x 18 high; A 2154 yd (1969 m), B 480 yd (438 m), C 1320 yd (1207 m), D 480 yd (438 m)	Ch349; repeats = 85 wide x 23 high; A 3928 yd (3591 m), B 874 yd (799 m), C 2413 yd (2206 m), D 874 yd (799 m)	A 834, B 1942, C 910a, D 816
Bibbledy Bobbledy Blue p.68	Ch125; repeats = 30 wide x 5 high; A 462 yd (422 m), B 68 yd (62 m), C 135 yd (123 m), D 133 yd (121 m)	Ch205; repeats = 50 wide x 10 high; A 1535 yd (1403 m), B 223 yd (203 m), C 445 yd (406 m), D 437 yd (399 m)	Ch289; repeats = 71 wide x 12 high; A 2613 yd (2389 m), B 378 yd (345 m), C 754 yd (689 m), D 742 yd (678 m)	A 847, B 820, C 903, D 851
Crossed Hatch p.70	Ch93; repeats = 45 wide x 7 high; A–E 170 yd (155 m) each	Ch153; repeats = 75 wide x 15 high; A–E 532 yd (486 m) each	Ch215; repeats = 106 wide x 19 high; A–E 934 yd (854 m) each	A 896, B 914a, C 827, D 1967, E 850
Flower Patch p.72	A 158 yd (144 m), B–E 237 yd (216 m) each, F 788 yd (720 m)	A 525 yd (480 m), B–E 788 yd (720 m) each, F 2625 yd (2400 m)	A 919 yd (840 m), B–E 1378 yd (1260 m) each, F 4594 yd (4200 m)	A 825, B 836, C 1941, D 1915, E 842, F 227
Folk Flower p.74	A–C 237 yd (216 m) each, D 335 yd (306 m), E 650 yd (594 m)	A–C 788 yd (720 m) each, D 1116 yd (1020 m), E 2166 yd (1980 m)	A–C 1378 yd (1260 m) each, D 1953 yd (1785 m), E 3790 yd (3465 m)	A 820, B 1952, C 851, D 914a, E 848
Knotty but Nice p.76	A 99 yd (90 m), B 237 yd (216 m), C 256 yd (234 m), D 197 yd (180 m), E 276 yd (252 m)	A 329 yd (300 m), B 788 yd (720 m), C 854 yd (780 m), D 657 yd (600 m), E 919 yd (840 m)	A 575 yd (525 m), B 1378 yd (1260 m), C 1493 yd (1365 m), D 1149 yd (1050 m), E 1608 yd (1470 m)	A 825, B 914a, C 1973, D 844, E 842